Advance praise for *Idea Agent*

"Straight from the career of a true leader in innovation, *Idea Agent* is timely, insightful, and practical. It points the way out of so many stifling corporate cultures and offers a realistic understanding of the brilliant, strong-minded, and fiercely rebellious creative personalities that baffle so many managers. A must-read for anyone serious about stoking the flames of innovation in their company."

—Rob Kaiser, President, Kaiser Leadership Solutions, Senior Partner, Kaplan DeVries Inc., and author, *The Versatile Leader* (with Bob Kaplan) and *The Perils of Accentuating the Positive*

"*Idea Agent* is the perfect book for anyone managing smart, creative, energetic people. Lina Echeverría has done just that—and gotten great work from them. *Idea Agent* is filled with real-life stories of how innovation works at the front lines of the economy today. Echeverría is a great guide to supporting people whose very brilliance often makes them a challenge inside traditional workplaces. You'll come away from this book with a whole set of tools and examples to give your own teams both creativity and focus."

—Charles Fishman, *New York Times* bestselling author of *The Wal-Mart Effect* and *The Big Thirst* and long-time staff member at *Fast Company* magazine

"Most books overlook the fact that real innovation goes beyond simple processes and techniques. With her unassailable credibility as someone who has done it in an American powerhouse of innovation, who knows what it is like, and who was extremely successful, Echeverría shows us that sustained innovation comes from developing cultures that inspire, impassion, and empower others to explore, act, and take risks on new possibilities. Creativity and innovation come from the inside out not from the outside in. Lina shows us the way well."

—Clint Sidle, Director, Roy H. Park Leadership Fellows Program, Johnson Graduate School of Management, Cornell University, and author, *The Leadership Wheel* and *This Hungry Spirit*

"As a collaborator and witness, I have seen Lina's leadership philosophy in action, focusing the talents of brilliant, colorful—and sometimes obstreperous—characters, gaining their trust and fostering the synergy across the enterprise that led to historic innovations. In *Idea Agent* she shows us that innovation is not a question of just assembling talent and providing resources, but of creating an environment where the individuals' entire selves can be leveraged in a collaborative process. This book is not for the aspiring executive who sees leadership as a means of self-glorification, but rather for those who understand that leadership is service and responsibility to the organization with potential that surpasses any one individual (or one's own self). I have watched the insights articulated in this engrossing book in action, and they work!"

— Peter L. Bocko, CTO, Glass Technologies Group,
Corning Incorporated

"Anyone interested in creating breakthrough innovations will benefit from reading this book—a deeply personal, authentic, and moving chronicle of one woman's quest for innovation in one of the most creative places in the world. This is not yet another theoretical text on creativity and innovation in the workplace; rather, it takes the reader on a rich journey through the trenches of one woman's real-life experiences and hard-won, often surprising, insights regarding how to foster innovation in a large, global organization."

— Susan M. Cantrell, Research Fellow at Accenture's Institute for
High Performance Business and author, *Workforce of One:
Revolutionizing Talent Management Through Customization*

"*Idea Agent* is a beautifully written and highly engaging exploration of innovation leadership. Filled with deeply personal stories and insights from Lina Echeverría's distinguished career as an innovation leader at Corning, I know of no other book that better deals with the human side of innovation."

— Dean R. Spitzer, Ph.D., innovation expert and author,
Transforming Performance Measurement

IDEA AGENT

IDEA AGENT

Leadership That Liberates Creativity
and Accelerates Innovation

Lina M. Echeverría

American Management Association

New York • Atlanta • Brussels • Chicago • Mexico City • San Francisco
Shanghai • Tokyo • Toronto • Washington, D.C.

Bulk discounts available. For details visit:
www.amacombooks.org/go/specialsales
Or contact special sales:
Phone: 800-250-5308
E-mail: specialsls@amanet.org
View all the AMACOM titles at: www.amacombooks.org
American Management Association: www.amanet.org

This publication is designed to provide accurate and authoritative information in regard to the subject matter covered. It is sold with the understanding that the publisher is not engaged in rendering legal, accounting, or other professional service. If legal advice or other expert assistance is required, the services of a competent professional person should be sought.

With the exception of Dasa, all names that appear in the text are noms de guerre, and some details have been modified for identity protection. Otherwise, all circumstances are true to the best of the author's recollection.

Library of Congress Cataloging-in-Publication Data

Echeverría, Lina M.
   Idea agent : leadership that liberates creativity and accelerates innovation /
Lina M. Echeverría.
     p.   cm.
   Includes index.
   ISBN 978-0-8144-3217-4 (hardcover)
   1. Creative ability in business.   2. Self-actualization (Psychology)
3. Leadership.   I. Title.

   HD53.E24 2012
   658.4'092—dc23

                                                                    2012015318

About AMA
American Management Association (www.amanet.org) is a world leader in talent development, advancing the skills of individuals to drive business success. Our mission is to support the goals of individuals and organizations through a complete range of products and services, including classroom and virtual seminars, webcasts, webinars, podcasts, conferences, corporate and government solutions, business books, and research. AMA's approach to improving performance combines experiential learning—learning through doing—with opportunities for ongoing professional growth at every step of one's career journey.

Printing number
10 9 8 7 6 5 4 3 2 1

For Colin and Maia,
my reason for it all

CONTENTS

FOREWORD

ASK ANY CEO or organizational leader for a list of those things that keep them up at night and *innovation* will be at or near the top of the list. The reasons for this are easily understandable. Large firms, often with a long and proud tradition, are failing at an alarming rate. Kodak, founded 125 years ago, is in bankruptcy. Sears, long America's dominant retailer, is in a slow-motion liquidation, closing stores and selling off brands. General Motors, the largest company in America in 1959, was bankrupt fifty years later. The list of failed firms, including Borders Books, the Tribune, Blockbuster, Merrill Lynch, Circuit City, and a host of banks and airlines, goes on. Studies have shown that the average life expectancy of a Standard and Poor's company is now about twelve years. Only 37 percent of firms on the Fortune 500 list in 1957 were around forty years later. In a study of the world's largest companies between 1912 and 1995, an economic historian found that only twenty survived over this period—and that they were firms in industries like natural resources that had not been subject to disruptive change.

Faced with this reality, leaders of companies appreciate how important it is for their organizations to innovate if they are going to survive. But knowing that innovation is essential is not the same thing as actually doing it. How can leaders drive innovation within their organizations? This book offers inspiring and practical insights to this question.

The fundamental tension facing leaders of innovation is to promote both *creativity* and *execution*—to come up with new ways of doing things and to ensure that these new ideas are implemented. It is only when new ideas are developed and implemented that we say someone or something is innovative. Many organizations have been creative in that they developed new technologies and products, but failed because they were unable to successfully introduce these new ideas into the marketplace (think Xerox Parc with the personal computer, EMI with the original CAT scanner, or Kodak with the first digital camera). Other companies have excelled at the execution of ideas but ultimately failed when they were unable to come up with new products and services (think Blockbuster and its inability to rent DVDs by mail, the failure of U.S. Steel to adjust to lower-cost steel produced by mini-mills, or how formerly great airlines like Pan Am and TWA were unable to adjust to newer, low-cost competition). The challenge for leaders is to foster both creativity and execution—to promote both freedom and discipline.

There is no shortage of advice for how to do this. While many innovation books are filled with insight and practical advice, most suffer from a certain clinical detachment that fails to realistically capture the passion as well as the rigor that real innovation requires. Many authors who study innovation and change (myself included) do a credible job of describing the challenges leaders face in generating innovation within organizations. On occasion, we may also offer reasonable suggestions for how leaders can enhance innovation. What we don't do, however, is to fully capture the passion and complexity that these suggestions require. We are like music critics describing a symphonic performance, not the conductor or musician who actually makes it happen, or the historian who describes great battles but has never fought in one. In this sense, our prescriptions, while technically correct, fail to get at the heart of what it really takes to succeed—to be a symphony conductor or a combat leader. Unlike the authors of many books about organizational innovation who study but never practice what they preach, Lina Echeverría has actually done it.

Lina has been there and truly understands what it takes to make both creativity and execution come alive. Her experience has given her the understanding of the delicate balance, the "creative tension," between unleashing creative researchers and harnessing their work to actual products and revenues—and has made her uniquely qualified to capture it in writing. Lina is first a world-renowned engineer and scientist with a Ph.D. in geology and over thirty years of experience as both a scientist and a senior manager at Corning—a 150-year-old company with a distinguished history of technical innovation and organizational transformation that has produced everything from optical fiber to pollution controls for cars to the windows in NASA spacecraft to the durable screens in smartphones. Aside from her numerous technical achievements (patents and publications), Lina has managed scientists and technical professionals in Europe and the United States. In her role as a vice president for science and technology at Corning, she was responsible for developing new technologies and converting these into successful products—the essence of creativity and execution. Over her career, she has led research efforts and delivered technologies in areas as diverse as ceramics, telecommunications, fiber optics, nanotechnology, and liquid crystal displays. To accomplish this, she has led everything from small teams to entire R&D laboratories. Throughout her career she has developed a reputation as a leader who is able to bring out the very best in her subordinates while creating an atmosphere of creativity and excitement. She has done all this while raising two successful children (both scientists) and pursuing her own artistic passions for textiles and creating "wearable art." Just as a small example of her energy and passion, while working as a scientist, she conducted field research on the small island that was the site of Colombia's highest security prison—and she did this while living in a tropical rainforest and carrying her 6-month old baby on her back.

Her experiences as a world-renowned scientist and manager give her insight and empathy not available to those who simply observe and describe. They allow her to capture both the emotions, the triumphs, and the failures involved in helping organizations innovate. In doing this, she also offers pragmatic suggestions for dealing with the tensions involved in leading a creative organization. This is not second-hand knowledge gained through interviews and stories but real insight into the creative process. Her book is both a fascinating memoir and the distillation of her experience into relevant management lessons. It conveys an important message that is too often lost in other books about managing innovation: Leading innovation is more than an intellectual exercise. It is about conflict, psychology, and passion—what she refers to as "the seven passions" of innovation. Her rich stories and examples make the process come alive and capture the nuances that other treatments so often miss. These offer a far more vibrant and memorable picture than other books—and help the reader really see what it takes to become a leader of innovation in organizations.

Charles O'Reilly
Frank E. Buck Professor of Management and Director,
Leading Change and Organizational Renewal Executive Program,
Stanford Graduate School of Business
Author, *Winning Through Innovation: A Practical Guide to Leading Organizational Change and Renewal* and *Ambidextrous Organizations: Resolving the Innovator's Dilemma*, both with M. Tushman, and *Hidden Value: How Great Companies Achieve Extraordinary Results with Ordinary People*, with J. Pfeffer

IDEA AGENT

Leadership for Fast-Paced Innovation

IT IS APPARENT to all those engaged in the work of developing and industrializing technology that the world of innovation is competitive and fast-moving, and true innovation must be "ahead of the facts" to provide sustainable differentiation. The last century witnessed the transformation of our lives through advancements—in technology, in medicine, in cinematography, in architecture—based on the delivery of what, relative to the challenges confronted today, could be considered the "easy stuff." As we look at the nineteenth and twentieth centuries, it is not an overstatement to say that the inventions then were simpler than what we are facing today, simpler in that they relied on one scientific or technical discipline, addressed immature or nonexistent markets waiting to be developed, or responded to human needs eager to be satisfied. From the invention of the light bulb or the discovery of penicillin and the subsequent development of antibiotics, or the invention of film, to the germination of the Internet through the delivery of optical fiber, breakthroughs could rely on the genius of one inventor and the work of essentially unidisciplinary teams. Winning in today's world requires not only unique insight and real creativity, but demands multidisciplinary teams delivering together. With this complexity and high pace, normal innovation processes are necessary but not sufficient to generate real breakthroughs.

Today, breakthrough innovation is brutally difficult and growing more so by the day. Not only are major inventions increasingly complex and being developed at an accelerating rate, but to be first to market and attain a sustainable advantage, innovators must be able to anticipate needs and intuit solutions while working in high-powered multidisciplinary teams. This is where the key lies. Bringing the team to perform in symphony is what drives innovation. And it starts with understanding the difference between creativity and innovation. As beautifully described by Teresa Amabile, creativity is the confluence of a capacity for approaching situations in an imaginative way and the mastery of the skills required and the passion to make it happen. It is an *essential element* to innovation. Innovation is making a breakthrough happen and see the light in a concrete way. But creativity, by itself, does not produce innovation. Leading teams to deliver innovation is what leads to the breakthrough, and it is a skill all its own, which, like the high-performance instrument it is, cannot be generalized with organizational programs. It must be fine-tuned daily, case by case, one person at a time.

Creativity needs to thrive every day at the front lines of organizations between groups with diverging cultures. Researchers and business leaders at technology companies, artists and executives at film studios, surgeons and managers at hospitals: these cultures clash on a daily basis. It is imperative to balance freedom and rigor by giving the creatives the freedom to find path-breaking new ideas while imposing the kind of rigor that business and competition, budgets, and product cycles require. You need to have both—and you can. The secret successful enterprises know is that harnessing creativity requires researchers, developers, manufacturers, and marketers working together, rather than constantly battling over goals and priorities.

An impassioned culture of innovation thrives when guided by leaders who can resonate with team members, leaders capable of managing with passion and creating energized organizations while staying true to themselves and making their own work meaningful. Innovation thrives under a leader who internalizes and lives by the belief that to excel you must start with a group; to excel you must create a culture; and to excel you must manage one by one—one person at a time, one situation at a time, one project at a time, one group at a time—by staying in the present, undistracted.

As leaders we must maximize our ability to draw out the full potential of our best performers and coax from them the driving force to make it happen. Getting to know the creative personalities—their personal passions, their idiosyncrasies and strengths—is a priority in delivering breakthrough innovation. Equally important is the priority of managing the conflict that will inevitably result from the interaction of strong creative personalities. These are two key everyday practices to "managing those who reject management" and to deliver results, for innovation is no accident. We need to manage, motivate, and inspire; to tap intuition and hunches; to use feelings of laughter, anger, and sadness to elicit the inexplicable. We need to create a culture that understands creativity—the ability to have a vision and the way to materialize it—while providing the space for it to flourish and to yield. Above all we need to manage this passion with passion. Managing with passion is neither about unproductive freewheeling nor boxing in and controlling. It is about creating a culture that liberates passion and frees up creativity, that sets high expectations while creating "negative space" where intuition can flow.

For decades, the world of managing for innovation has been fertile research ground. Put the words "creativity," "innovation," and "management" in a literature search and you will get the impression that the number of publications—and, hence, research activities—on these subjects is growing exponentially. Authors discuss the paucity of truly innovative people, and significant effort has been devoted to defining what innovators look like. From these observations comes research on the challenges of fitting innovators within organizations because they have a low boredom threshold, they do not want to be led, and they ignore corporate hierarchy and expect instant access. And naturally, the process followed by innovators receives considerable attention, with the innovator proposing, experts opining with conflicting opinions, the innovator seeing critical components and their connections and finally bridging different parts to recombine pieces and cultivate buy-in for innovation.

Research on the nature of the creative mind and the process it favors often constitutes the basis for studies leading to recommendations for managing for creativity. While acknowledging that companies often stifle their creative talent by leaving it hidden in the working trenches and instead end up developing carbon-copy leaders who don't innovate, recommendations often focus on establishing strong, clearly articulated, and clearly implemented leadership competency models: talent management processes that put identified innovators in the line of fire, where they are expected to thrive, and surround them with mentors and peer network for support.

There is no final assessment on whether recommendations that address the needs of an organization by proposing *more* organizational processes work or not, but it is apparent that they are not jump-starting innovation. Perhaps we need to look at inventions past and present, understand what the world needs, and manage for the ultimate need: delivery of breakthroughs.

This is not a theoretical book summing up research. Instead it is a personal chronicle of my experience in leading creative talent and delivering technology through developing human beings, and of being equally impacted by them. The challenges imposed by creative personalities, "rogues" juxtaposed with "good corporate citizens"; the demands of leading conflicted personalities and big egos; and the tension between creative freedom and management rigor forged me and led me to understand who I needed to become as a leader in order to serve them as human beings and deliver breakthroughs together. Whereas from researchers such as Tushman and O'Reilly readers learn about how ambidextrous organizations can achieve both efficiency and innovation, in these pages I simply portray what the real tension between these two forces—creative freedom and management rigor—feels like from the trenches of innovation efforts.

We are all different, and I trust that my experience will apply to many individuals regardless of their specific situation. It is my intention to inspire anyone interested in leading groups responsible for creativity and innovation by identifying with the narration and applying it to her particular situation. The different stages from which I have lived the creative process and the reaction of different communities with whom these learnings have been shared are convincing evidence that the basics of human creativity and human interaction in organizations are essentially similar regardless of area of expertise. Inspiration, however, should not be taken to mean an effort of duplication, but a force for motivation. Thus my early exposure to creative people can be recreated by others by adopting wonder, openness, and respect for creative people and understanding their passion. And although my experience and the situations described were lived in an American powerhouse of industrial innovation, they apply just as well to fields ranging from architecture and the arts to the medical and biological sciences, in a wide variety of settings—from small entrepreneurial settings to large, complex organizations.

In my experience in technology innovation, management, and delivery, I have found seven essential elements that provide both the vibrancy and the rigor essential to create the culture of success in a team chartered with delivering innovation. I refer to these as Seven Passions of Innovation:

1. Looking at creative conflict in the eyes and flexing for resolution

2. Bringing together teams of diverse, highly intelligent people freely in a way that engages their deepest personal motivations

3. Living values that set creativity free

4. Insisting on excellence and results

5. Cultivating a culture that honors time for intuitive flow

6. Defining an organizational structure that guides, but allows solutions to come from many permutations of talent and function

7. Providing authentic leadership with the will to manage, the guts to decide, the wisdom to guide, and the passion to make innovation happen

These seven elements are not unarticulated components; rather they come together to make up a living system whose energy radiates from a leader at the core, its heart center. An impassioned leader with the detachment to remain centered. Around the leader gather the practitioners, embracing clearly defined values. The practices of leading through conflict, demanding excellence, and enriching lives create a culture where practitioners are enlivened and innovation thrives. The existence of a well-identified and recognized culture empowers the practitioners to express it beyond their own group and into the organization at large. This is a strong force for innovation, as energy shifts from the core outward through interactions with other groups, influencing the surrounding organization.

The Seven Passions of Innovation are no pixie dust. Transforming an organization by pursuing them takes a deep understanding of the creative spirit and of the needs of an organization to deliver; it takes strength, courage, and perseverance. And it takes the ability to be amazed and to have fun. They are an approach proven in the best corporate innovation settings to harness transforming creativity and drive group performance to its highest level. The Seven Passions are neither a recipe to be followed with specific ingredients added in sequence, but rather an approach and a philosophy meant as motivation and inspiration for every leader to create a culture where innovation thrives.

Conflict in Art and Science

MY FIRST ENCOUNTER with creative people was from the side-lines in my native Colombia. Creativity appeared in our lives and slowly, without our realizing it, became the dominant aspect of our household. In her forties, my mother—until then a housewife who enjoyed her role and was good at directing her cooks and other help to run a household—had taken an interest in art and the intellectual world. In her late teens and early twenties, she had taken art courses and was considering spending a few years in Italy to study it more seriously when the Second World War broke out. Now, after twenty years had gone by, she saw her interest blossom. She enrolled in an art institute, took lessons in the evenings, and befriended the local art community. It did not take long for our house to become the intellectual center of the city. My mother would often entertain Colombia's leading intellectuals and artists and their peers visiting from around the globe. Botero, the Colombian painter; Yevtushenko, the Russian poet; Mejía Vallejo and Oscar Hernández, the Colombian writers; and La Chunga, the Argentine dancer, all became household names for my siblings and me, who watched at first and interacted with them as we grew older.

They were not yet the highly recognized painters or laureate writers that they became, but their love for their activities, their ability to follow that inner voice, was palpable then. I have clear memories of passionate discussions, of acrid critiques, of excited reactions to new ideas or proposed techniques. The passions ran high, but no matter how extreme the opinion, there was room for it. And the characters would always come back the following day or week to start again. For these creative people—painters, novelists, sculptors, dancers, poets, art critics—the exchange was a source of energy and inspiration, the reaction from others a source of ideas.

These memories resonated in my mind when I entered the high-stakes world of corporate innovation and learned my first lessons about the importance of creating an environment where healthy conflict can thrive. I was hired in the early 1980s by Corning Incorporated, one of America's titans of innovation, with a history of accomplishment, from bringing Thomas Edison's light bulb to market to ushering in the telecommunications era by commercializing the first optical fibers, with a number of other world-changing inventions in between. At Corning I joined the core research group, which was chartered with exploring for the future. We were pretty much left alone, with little guidance or inspiration but with no opposition either. We fed on each other's ideas, and that was fine with us.

After three years in research, I was transferred into a development group and assigned to a project working on ceramic substrates for automotive emissions—cleaning engine emission gases before releasing them to the atmosphere. Corning, which had fifteen years of experience in ceramic substrates for emissions control for the automotive industry, was facing a fast pace of change in this industry, which demanded an equally fast response from the leader in substrates. The improvement of thermal shock resistance and the ability to control properties became a corporate priority. The project scientists were reliant on the theories that had been developed over the previous fifteen years, but a breakthrough was eluding them. As I joined the project, I looked at the substrates in a fresh way, using traditional techniques from my background in geology and coupling them with the understanding of glass-ceramics, a family of materials invented by a Corning scientist decades earlier.

My findings ran contrary to the established understanding, but rather than the dialogue or even passionate discussions I expected, I felt I was not given a fair hearing by anyone—not my teammates nor the senior scientists responsible for developing most of the theory. I was proposing a new hypothesis using techniques that were familiar to me, but, as always in science, there was no certainty that I was right. I was just being driven by a clear intuitive vision based on data I was generating. And the passion of that vision was my driving force. But I felt I was not given time during team meetings and that my views were not included by program managers in their technical summaries to management, and I saw my theories derided. Not finding support within the group and looking for a forum to put my hypotheses to the test in an atmosphere of open discussion and questioning—or continuing to lose my self-confidence—I sought the input and feedback of senior scientists in other parts of the lab. I discussed my hypotheses with senior glass scientists, joined forces with physicists and computer scientists to model the system, enlisted the support of the plant statistician to compare my data with that of years of plant production, and asked the support of the analytical personnel to test my hypotheses. Their analyses and discussions helped me gel my views and keep my sanity. I could clearly see the total picture, and I could understand the system well enough to be able to predict the results of experiments and subsequently prove them. I could feel the drive. And I predicted, and proved to my satisfaction on a small scale, that it was possible to achieve the challenging result that Corning needed: an increase in mechanical strength with a concomitant decrease in thermal expansion. I was having the rare experience that, much later as a seasoned manager, I would describe as "scientist on a roll."

Regardless of my efforts, I was not heard, and my frustration only deepened and my self-confidence eroded, shaken as much by my perceived low credibility with my teammates as by my own inability to establish a productive dialogue with them. So my request to Joe Sorelli, the project manager, was not for him to decree that my theories were right, but to give me equal discussion time, to at least back me up by giving credence to my background and expertise in the techniques I was introducing to the team. In other words: give me space, give me respect, give me support.

But Joe, a competent, jovial guy everybody—including me—liked, was baffled in trying to understand how difficult such a situation can be for a creative person. He was in the middle of two fires; my team members were coming to him as well, complaining that I could not take their critiques. And although it was easy for him to see the benefit of disagreement, an essential force in scientific pursuit, he had a harder time understanding when argument becomes unleashed as a force of destruction, when a creative person is being ostracized from an effort because of personal interactions, what happens when a leader fails to create an atmosphere of inclusion. Though not for lack of trying, Joe did not jump headlong into the fire. He did not deal with the forces of scientists who were passionate about their differing understanding of the system. And so he failed to create that much-needed atmosphere of inclusion and mutual respect.

My pain grew by the day. I started having unsettling recurring dreams of being exposed, unprotected, and surrounded. The message was clear. The gregarious Lina I knew did not even feel like attending group gatherings or office Christmas parties. So I did what most people with potential and gumption do under similar conditions: I looked for jobs outside Corning. It was a difficult decision, as my husband and I were a dual-career couple with young children nicely settled in their schools. But it was clear that my energy was gone and the gamble worth it. I had my first interview with a large company in Delaware when Donald Jameson, then manager of the glass research group, came down to my office to offer me a transfer into his group. The lab was a smaller community in the early 1980s than it is today, and managers knew people in other groups well. He had seen me make presentations during some of the exploratory project reviews, and no doubt the senior scientists I had consulted in developing my hypotheses gave him their views. He was throwing me a lifeline that I welcomed. And he capped it by offering me a position reporting to Mark Hewlett, a research fellow who not only was at the top of the technical echelon but was also an evolved soul and could bring perspective and wisdom to any situation in life from human to scientific, a wisdom that was to bring me much guidance and richness for decades to come. Yet it did not feel like a triumphal exit. "Your nose has been bloodied" was how the director of the development group described it. My confidence was shattered, my inspiration hijacked. My relief was peppered by shame as I moved on to new territory.

Some time later, when I was first given responsibility for a small group of scientists, it was apparent to me that I needed to create a culture where healthy conflict was more than valued and given space, but passionately engaged, as in the salons of my childhood. Though my experience of the opposite extreme had been painful, Joe Sorelli had given me my first lesson on the importance of managing for a level of healthy and productive conflict, one I would never forget. As I grew and started to manage technology delivery teams, getting to know the scientists, no longer as their peer but as their leader, all my childhood memories came back. It felt like déjà vu with a couple of changes: the setting was quite different, with state-of-the-art science and technology rather than art and literature as the subject matter, and with teams, rather than individual artists, as drivers. But there was something strongly reminiscent in the two worlds: the idiosyncrasies of the players, the intensity of their passion, the strength of their convictions, and, yes, the presence of strong egos. It felt very important to liberate that creativity and allow it to reach its potential, just as those artists and writers I had known had reached theirs, in contrast to my own first project experience. Furthermore, it felt important to learn to understand at what time argument—an essential force in scientific and creative discovery and advancement—becomes unhealthy. If a little conflict can be good and too much can be destructive, where is the break? How does a manager deal with a creative group that is becoming dysfunctional? These were the very questions Joe had grappled with and that, through his puzzlement, left an indelible mark on me. Many years would go by before we exchanged views during my process of writing, when he would recollect for me: "Your work was a very big success. Your inventiveness and your tenacity forced others to look differently at a situation, and knowledge was advanced. Nonetheless, in this process you were made to feel unwelcome, disrespected, and disowned. The project was a technical success, but we lost a creative member of the team; the company almost lost you and you were miserable, and no one should be made to feel that way. I acknowledge that this was a management failure. I would not, however, like you to think it was for lack of trying."

So, in my mind, the question was how to create a model where there could be room for all opinions? Where the characters would always come back to start again? Where the exchange could be a source of energy and inspiration, and the reaction from others a source of ideas? Where ego and pride do not get in the way? Where conflicts get resolved and there would never be anyone who did not come back?

Unlikely as it may seem—years later I would have responsibility for the groups delivering research in this very area, and, in an effort at fairness and impartiality, I stayed away from what had been my own research—I would have to wait almost a quarter-century to find out that my ideas had been incorporated into the work that followed. As I was about to retire after a draining battle with aggressive breast cancer, Luke Papadakis, the plant statistician I had consulted back then—somebody whose openness of mind and scientific curiosity had always made me feel comfortable—came to my retirement celebration and, with some pain, shared his experience. He explained how, based on my understanding of the system and my proposed firing schedules, they have learned how to do it right and the plant can now tailor the system to deliver a broad range of properties.

A year later, when touching base with players for accuracy and consent for this manuscript, Joe Sorelli would say to me: "Your discovery, which I maintain was one of the most important discoveries in that technology, allowed us to optimize firing schedules from the point of understanding how to control crystal size and microcracking. This was used in both substrate and filter processes, especially when new compositions were developed. Your ideas greatly influenced the work that continued. I suspect that you never got the proper recognition for your work. I tried to rectify that in my 'legends' talk, but too little and too late. The failure was the effect on you and on the team effort. When it was over, the team had lost a creative and valuable member and wasted a lot of energy making heat rather than light. In the end, of course, your efforts became a big success and you should feel good about it. Furthermore, the fundamental understanding you elicited was a big deal. It would have been a great scientific paper, but for proprietary reasons, we would never have allowed it to be published—too valuable."

I was reminded, once again, of why it is important for leaders to give space to the passion that drives creatives, for they "know without knowing why" and they can be ahead of the curve that leads to opportunities. And, yes, Joe is right: today I do feel good about it—though back then all I could feel was the extinction of my creative fire. And now, I cannot help but think of the last lines of Hemingway's *The Sun Also Rises:* "We could have had such a damned good time together . . ."

Into the Ring of Fire

AS ANYONE WHO HAS BEEN SURROUNDED by creative artists, writers, or musicians knows, creativity often comes along with strong—even conflicted—personalities who will not stop in the face of obstacles along their way. The drive to materialize their vision is stronger than themselves, and today we enjoy the beauty they have created. Painters and writers such as Van Gogh and Hemingway come to mind. The former never sold a painting in his lifetime, and his wonderful contribution was cut short. The demons of the latter were never conquered, and we are left to wonder what he left unsaid. But even when the best of circumstances are provided, the personalities, the egos, the insecurities, the jealousies, create conflict. Though the world created by the Medicis was enviable to anyone outside its aura, even the two creative geniuses sheltered by it, Michelangelo and Da Vinci, could not escape the sting of rivalry.

KNOW AND UNDERSTAND CREATIVES

Creativity can be a hot fire and you have to love it to gain from it. Fear of managing the passions of creative scientists will only lead to missed opportunities. Not being afraid of moving to free up and channel the energy and the creativity, on the other hand, can open worlds of opportunities. But on most days, this does not feel comfortable. It is not about running teams that are always agreeable and polite, where everybody respects the turn of the other and the unexpected does not happen. It cannot be stressed enough: it is about understanding each one of the players for who they are, where they come from, what drives them, and what they can bring to the solution. And from this understanding, leadership that liberates creativity is about managing conflict—not preventing conflict from arising, but stepping into the ring of fire and managing all its actors and stages.

Double Duty
Balance Personalities to Realize Team Dynamics

Peter Murray, a forceful and creative scientist and one of my early hires as we expanded the glass research group to meet Corning's growth goals in the mid-1990s, personifies the hot fire of creativity. A midcareer hire from one of the national labs, his zeal for all things was palpable from the first day of his interview. His interests were broad and he excelled in everything he did, from playing classical piano, to understanding complex glass systems and predicting their behavior as their composition changed, to cooking any cuisine or debating on any subject. Bright, articulate, and forceful, his presence was felt as he walked into any room. Feedback from some during his interview process was, "He is too good for Corning. He won't last long." It was clear that he was a winner, but it was also clear that we had a good challenge in our hands if we wanted him—and Corning—to succeed.

I assigned him to a project addressing a manufacturing issue in Corning's U.S. display glass plant. Years earlier, Corning had developed a process for making the highest quality ultra-thin glass in the market, used today to manufacture specialized thin glass for display purposes ranging from large-area LCD screens to laptop computers and smartphones. With the world's voracious appetite for large-area displays, the applications continued to expand, and with them the need to develop new glass compositions to meet new needs. When we hired Peter, Corning was beginning to open what was then a new market space that today represents a leading business for the corporation.

LCD precision glass, a premium product designed to have semiconductors and color filters deposited directly on it, has strict requirements that do not tolerate flaws on its surface. One defect capable of blocking a single pixel on a meter-wide sheet of glass renders the entire sheet unacceptable. In contrast with today, when Corning has manufacturing plants in four different countries and a great deal of flexibility for process development, in the mid-1990s it relied almost exclusively on one U.S. plant for its process development and for a large portion of its supply of product. At the time this was one of only two plants in the world devoted to the manufacture of ultra-thin specialty glass for display applications. And it had been experiencing a manufacturing upset that caused the glass to grow tiny crystals, surface flaws that rendered the huge glass sheets unacceptable. We had struggled with the issue in research and in manufacturing, and as Peter joined the team, his new ideas started flowing, expressed in his unique and forceful way and leaving little room for the voices of other team members to be heard. He had a vision, the experience to back it, and the ability to roll over all other team members with his arguments. Other team members, with alternative views and softer styles or shorter appetites for active engagement, could not make their voices heard. He represented the research part of the equation and was willing to take on development and manufacturing. It was clear that he had the knowledge and experience that could lead us to a solution, so the question was twofold: Could the team survive with him? And could we survive without him?

BE COMFORTABLE AROUND CONFLICT AND ADDRESS IT DEFTLY

The creative and the passionate are difficult to manage. Their strong egos drive them to make their vision a reality even if this means creating conflict, which can happen even under the best of circumstances. Leading a creative team means harnessing this conflict and managing it to benefit, not detract from, the work. Even if your larger corporate culture does not encourage, reward, or even tolerate much disagreement or dispute, it is your job as manager to create a space where it is safe to challenge teammates, to argue, to disagree, and ultimately to seek a better, more robust answer.

If creative beings can be conflicted internally, just think of the conflict that can arise when strong creative personalities, with different approaches or visions driven by their own creativity, are brought together as a team. You will have divergences, clashes, and tension. And if you have not experienced it, perhaps the level of control in your organization is high enough that the dissent is being discouraged. But then so are the good ideas, the ones that come at a ninety-degree angle from your planned path. Attempting to stay on or manage from the sidelines will keep you there: on the sidelines and far from the goal. As a leader, it starts with you knowing your people, their reactions and expectations, their roles in the team. There are different-colored tools on your palette to use at your discretion, starting with the self-management resulting from self-awareness. An understanding of each human being and the way he or she relates to others needs to be your guide. It continues with being comfortable with conflict and with understanding that arguments and discussion are as essential to science as experimentation itself. And it moves on with playing an active role in managing conflict, literally sitting at the negotiating table rather than shying away from it.

In Peter's case, I weighed the options: playing the roles of functional and project leader simultaneously—a less-than-ideal long-term solution—or adding a scientist to the team with the sole purpose of easing the tension and improving the communication between main players, or bringing in a guru with a Buddhist approach to help team members move into awareness. As a leader, the need to jump into the fire and manage conflict was imperative.

Because of the gravity of the manufacturing issue, which was preventing us from delivering Corning's first new composition for an emerging market, and because of the potential that was evident in Peter as a contributor, it was necessary to pull out all the stops. Knowing him well enough to understand his intellectual capabilities, strong personality, and need for respect and recognition, and as the functional manager for the glass research, I took on the role of project leader to ensure a forceful presence that would create space for all voices to be heard. It was important to be strong but thoughtful and accepting, to be inspirational without losing rigor. Though it was not a sustainable long-term solution, I ran the project, convened meetings, set the agenda, and defined timelines. But most importantly, on a day-to-day basis, I was responsible for the dynamics of communication, for weighing in on different arguments, for making sure that the floor was clear for open debate and that opinions were heard and discussed, and, most importantly, that Peter's driving force guided the project while preventing the force of his personality from steamrolling others.

As those who have transferred technology from research to manufacturing know, it was also important to maintain strong communication between the research group and the development and manufacturing groups. But Peter's strong personality and superior knowledge of glass science had brought out all the insecurities of Chris Cunningham, the glass scientist responsible for the technology transfer between research and manufacturing. Now in the development group, Chris had been one of the first scientists to ever report to me when I was first made a research supervisor. A solid glass scientist with good practical experience and a proven record of invention of glass composition, he had a sense of ownership of the compositional area applicable to display glasses, having worked under the pioneer in this field of glass research. But trained in the practical tradition of glass science rather than having the sophisticated theoretical background that Peter possessed, Chris saw in Peter a major threat, and he reacted accordingly, with both active and passive resistance. A quiet personality, Chris had a rich personal life and devoted much of his time outside the lab to his farm, an activity shared and enjoyed by a handful of other scientists in the glass research group who saw Corning's location in rural upstate New York as an opportunity to follow their passions inside and outside the lab.

There was a small community of "scientist-farmers" with common interests who shared concerns and trusted each other. And it was this connection that provided the key to solving the team communication issues. I asked Rick Laredo, a glass researcher who was a member of the scientist-farmer community with a good relationship with Chris, to join the team, with the sole purpose of improving the communication between research and development. I explained clearly the situation to him and my expectation of him.

The assignment was unconventional: scientists are supposed to do science, not personnel development—that is the domain of human resources. It also carried a risk. Without a specific technical responsibility, what would Rick have to show as his results for the time invested at the end of the year? I had been managing the glass research group for more than a year, and there was already a culture of common goals, of pitching in, of making things happen together. The risk of not developing a manufacturing solution was greater for the whole, and Rick came on board. Already enjoying the trust and personal friendship of Chris, he soon established a close relationship between the research and the development group, who welcomed his addition to the team and felt the relief of having a go-between. But my responsibility to create the space and opportunities for Rick to continue to develop his own work, his personal career, his sense of worth, was not one that I could take lightly. I had to make sure that his role as communicator within the team was neither all-consuming nor too long-lasting, that he would have the space to create and investigate on his own, part of the time during the assignment and back to full attention in a short time. Jointly, we balanced both requirements, and so in time Rick Laredo became the father of glass-binding technology at Corning.

Chris pursued a different path, moving on to the customer interface and becoming over time one of the display industry's most influential glass technology advocates. In his soft-spoken way, and always armed with a solid understanding, he became a reassuring presence for customers as they adapted the new glasses demanded by new applications in display technologies.

The goal was not—and it never should be—to eliminate the discussions or to shy away from disagreements and heated arguments. Instead the goal is to capture the energy of disparate viewpoints and use it to move the team forward rather than slowing it down. Though it was draining on my energy and my time—my full-time job was to lead the glass research group—I continued to manage the team, and the discussions were passionate. We did not shy away from conflict or try to suppress it. It was a long, arduous project, tackling a difficult problem. The cast of characters was large, from research to development, engineering, and manufacturing. In the end, the solution required input from all sides: glass compositions were changed, manufacturing processes readjusted, engineering modifications to the equipment made. But we had achieved a state of "creative conflict," which allowed all the voices to be heard, and thus we were able to find a robust solution.

With these two elements of project management and team dynamics addressing the main issues, the team went on to deliver a solution to the specific manufacturing issue. This enabled Corning to open a market and enabled the world to enjoy large-scale manufacturing of LCD television displays of increasingly larger sizes. More importantly, Peter's energy and contagious enthusiasm allowed him to gain the trust of the manufacturing community, which eventually yielded to his pressure to test new conditions that would allow an ever-widening world of glass compositions to be made into high-precision flat glass. The world of display and telecommunication products that we see today owes a debt to that insistence by one outspoken scientist, expressing his opinions assertively and insisting on maintaining high technical standards, who was not shut down by his environment.

For me this was a reassuring conclusion to what had been months of highly visible, intense effort—even participating by teleconference in daily meetings with the glass composition team and the manufacturing community during my family vacations in Colombia—where I was leading by following my intuition and common sense. For, as young managers everywhere know, there are no "how to" manuals, and for me, as well as for many others, it was "learn as you go." One at a time, I had started to place the bricks for a good foundation.

Managing conflict and tempers, however, does not mean compromising. Yes, it would indeed be much easier to allow the superstars in your group to get their way. It would seem a natural reward for their contributions. But it does not foster the culture of accountability that is critical for trust. And, just as the "domestiques"—the "support" members of a Tour de France cycling team whose role is to put the star on the podium at the end of the grueling three-week race—need to trust their leader to give for him all the power in their legs during those hard Alpine climbs, so does the technology delivery team need trust to follow what might appear to be a harebrained idea. So as leaders, we must demand mutual respect and create a culture of accountability — starting with our own and making no exceptions. For the best scientific intellects are also capable of the highest levels of ethical behavior. So even if the delivery is painful, do not compromise.

The Crown Jewel of Tools
Self-Management Through Awareness

With the display technologies unit's manufacturing issue solved, it would have been simple to call it a job well done. But the ultimate goal of creating a culture where innovation thrives and delivers would elude us, and, just as important, Peter's development as a total being and the potential in his career would not be well served. It was just as important for him to gain the awareness of his role in the conflict and its solution. That is where the guru comes into play.

His name was Dasa and I first encountered him as he led a group of managers through a workshop in providing 360-degree feedback to employees during their annual performance evaluation. It was my first year as a manager and I found the information useful and his focus on self-awareness very insightful. I began calling on him to help me support the group on management of conflict. With a Ph.D. in history from Yale and years of experience on the Cornell faculty, he was a vast resource on the literature of workplace leadership, high performance, philosophy, psychology, and the like. His passion was in the actualization of human potential in the workplace and, even though conflict management was not his preferred area, bringing awareness to leaders and employees was part of his path.

This part of conflict management, of leading individuals through the process of gaining awareness, is not easy. Nor is it instantaneous. It requires insight, perseverance, and, overall, a willingness to gain awareness. Fundamentally, it starts with an agreement that there is an interest in the process, continues with a collection of feedback on the behavior of the individual and its effect on others, and follows with a series of coaching sessions. The duration of the relationship is determined by the appetite of the individual. I was working with Dasa myself after gaining the understanding that the first quality of a leader is self-awareness. My own work on self-awareness with Dasa went on for many years. Peter's relationship with this work had more of a seesaw quality to it.

From this work Peter learned that he was received for what he was: a creative researcher, frequently offering useful ideas and suggestions, and coming up with new approaches to difficult problems. He learned that he was viewed as energetic, displaying contagious enthusiasm and having a positive effect on his colleagues. That he enjoyed collaboration with other scientists and that he had demonstrated an interest and ability to mentor younger scientists was also apparent. These were not surprises to him, and neither was it a surprise to learn that he was outspoken, expressed his opinions assertively, and helped to maintain high technical standards. The focus of the work for Peter was the awareness that the same qualities that made him a powerful source of positive energy would at times swing back and result in behavior that negated his valuable technical contributions. Perhaps the biggest surprise for him was that even though he was seen as a positive element in challenging the status quo and in removing barriers to his and others' contributions, his exuberant energy was overwhelming to colleagues with more sedate personalities. From his self-assured vantage point, he had not been sensitive to this.

Peter started to work on modulating the oscillations and keeping his energy centered around more even behavior patterns. A few months later, feedback indicated that the beginning of a positive change was already recognizable. This was just the beginning of his process, and work continued on and off, as he was ready, over long periods of time. There were results; he was worth it and both Corning and he were gaining. Today, nearly fifteen years after that first interview, Peter's multiple contributions to new technology developments have been recognized and he has been promoted to research fellow, the highest rung of the technical ladder at Corning.

Patterns of behavior are imprinted on us throughout our lives, starting early on, conditioning us in ways we may not recognize but that drive our reaction to daily exchanges. Our role as leaders is to guide our people to maintain an effort to reach awareness for as long as they have the drive. And this is where our wisdom as leaders lies: in creating the space for this exploration while knowing our people well enough to walk with those who are ready for the search, but not push those who are not driven to venture into it; and, of course, to model the way by getting to know ourselves deeply and having the awareness of how our own style and reactions affect those around us. But it is not an effort that yields results instantly. It is an effort that yields deep and tangible results for the organization and for the individuals who constitute it.

FIND YOUR COURAGE

Conflict is expressed in many ways, affecting the daily lives of team members, defining the way they interact, influencing the culture of the organization, and having an effect on projects and results. And having the guts, the resilience, and the perseverance to address it has a dominant influence on the culture of the organization. If left unaddressed, conflict has the power to overcome all efforts in creating a positive environment, for it can polarize teams, erode self-confidence, and shatter motivation. The elements of resolution need to be as unique as the human beings involved, and there is no one-size-fits-all approach. The effort involved can swing from the few moments that it takes to stop by somebody's office to months of involvement. It is the passion to jump into the fire and address conflict that creates the culture of trust that is at the core of a resonant, successful organization. Trust that you will be given space. Trust that you will be heard. Trust that you are supported. Trust that there is accountability for senior and junior members. Trust creates a winning situation, for it is returned with willingness to pitch in, to make an extra effort, to give back to the leader for the searing that the fire might impart.

Managing personalities and tempers is not fun. It takes courage, serenity, flexibility, and tact. Courage to understand that managing tempers does not mean compromising and that creating untouchable personalities means eroding the culture you are trying to create: the culture of respect, accountability, and trust that drives the group. Serenity to stay detached during your exchanges. Flexibility to treat each personality in the unique way that is fruitful for each person involved. And tact to find the way to deliver a message in a way that does not flare tempers but yields results.

All Must Rise

The Significance of Engaging Rogues

Paul Genetti was a seasoned physicist blessed with a bright intellect, a charismatic personality, and wide-ranging interests, from literature, to dancing and volleyball. He had to his name the largest number of patents in the technology group, and had risen and established himself as an influential force in the lab. Already a research fellow, he had the freedom to initiate projects of his choosing and to express his opinion on any subject, both of which he did with gusto. He was proud to declare that he "could not be managed," and, whether out of respect or intimidation, management left him alone. His forceful influence was not only expressed, but also felt—and anticipated—by the lab.

I had gotten to know him early in my career, and we developed mutual appreciation and respect as we got to know each other through long conversations in his office. His area of research was glass, so he interacted with our scientists and swayed scientific opinions as much as feelings. Because of this interaction, he was an unofficial member of our group, and because of his influence, it was important for me that he embraced our values and exhibited similar behaviors. But he did not report to me. On one occasion, I was advised that Paul, while having an argument with one of the patent attorneys over a patent being drafted for one of his inventions, had lost his fiery temper and manhandled the attorney verbally. "It was just a Paul moment," seemed to be the general perception, and he was left alone.

My reaction, as well as that of the patent department director, was that it was unacceptable. It was not a way of expressing the respect, trust, and other values important to an organization nor a way of modeling behavior for younger scientists. In terms of conflict, this was not a difficult situation. The only difficulty

was the persona of the doer. Resolution only took two office visits, one from me, the second one from him.

My immediate goal was for Paul to mend the relationship and
re-establish his personal bridge to the patent department. But
the overarching goal was for Paul to see himself in the leadership position that he had established for himself and not in the
rebel-without-a-cause position that he held dear, to have him
develop the awareness of his behavior and the understanding
that, at work, success depends on the mutual reliance of a collaborative group, one reaching from the research to the patent
department. And to take that awareness one step further to
embrace the concept of magnanimous leadership, where an
apology, with the acceptance on the leader's part, only makes
him stronger. His intellect engaged in the discussion, and his spirit
followed. And he rose to the occasion.

Whereas Peter stretched my ability to be patient and challenged my persistence, Paul pushed me in a different way.
Resolving the tension that had been created required me to face
a situation that is more comfortably swept under the rug. But in
both cases, the sheer belief that I had in each of the players,
Peter and Paul, and in the value that they brought to the group, to
the culture, and to our goals, maintained my energy and my
determination. And my knowledge of them guided me in knowing
how far I could stretch them.

SUPPORT CREATIVES TO STAND ON THEIR OWN

Conflict often arises as two disparate personalities meet inside the
fighting ring, surrounded by spectators witnessing every move
and often weighing in with either support or critique for one side

or the other. Add to this spectacle the certainty of the scientific mind and the drive of the creative spirit and you have a spectacle charged with fire, a fire that if left unrestrained can be overpowering. In managing this fire the first approach that comes to mind is to tame the antagonistic element. But as leaders, our role is to serve and support people to succeed—all people, not just the belligerent ones. Yes, part of that role is to hold people accountable, not just for achieving results but for expressing respect for others through their behavior; another significant part is to support them in finding their driving force and freeing it up to channel their energy and creativity.

Finding Her Energy
A Path from Self-Awareness to Self-Assurance

Wendy Li was a soft, petite Asian American with a youthful, happy-go-lucky attitude who looked like she belonged on the runway more than in the halls of one of America's high-tech research labs. Shortly after hiring her, we assigned her to explore an exotic copper-based powdered glass for binding together sophisticated glass parts for photonic applications. She started experiencing difficulty establishing herself as a credible researcher when facing those whom she felt had a preconception of her as not "fitting the mold." The glass research group had a mix of characters and dispositions, and the towering figures and strong personalities shook Wendy's softer temperament. She did not feel openly welcomed by the "big guns" of strong-willed, temperamental, and forceful established celebrities she was facing. As she would express it after some years, she felt at the time that "there was not enough room in the hallways for their egos."

The path for me was clear: Rather than altering the makeup of the group or softening its vibrant temperament, it was important to work on shoring up Wendy's ability to push through on her own, on connecting to her inner drive and bringing it out as a source of strength. In a deeper context, this would free her up and allow her to channel her energy and creativity, and it would prepare her to face the strongest partners as well as rivals then and in her future. As I would often tell others, I knew I could not sanitize the world for her. But I could try to give her a strong immune system.

Through her inquiry under the guidance of Dasa, Wendy explored her issues of assertiveness, self-expression, and insecurities. She learned how her soft demeanor could be taken for a lack of strength, her happy attitude for a lack of purpose. And she had the determination to walk into the fire and address the core issues that held her back. As a tool of learning how to bring her inner strength of mind out as fortitude in her exchanges, Dasa suggested that she take up martial arts, which does just that: translate inner focus into outward, physical force. It was an intriguing approach, and she was open to pursue it. It did not take long before we could see her grow in her self-assurance, engage in arguments without backing out, begin to express herself assertively without losing the freshness and lightness that was hers. She delighted in her own ability to address specific behaviors and her own power to turn the situation around. It was indeed a wonderful and uplifting feeling for me to see her learn to spread her wings in a new dance. Today, after many years, she continues at Corning, happy in herself, strong in her delivery, having transformed herself and moved up to the commercial side of the organization, where she measures up in the toughest environments.

Some Things Never Change
Buttressing Careers Against Blockers

My first experience as a supervisor offered me a box-seat view of communication issues between two players. I only had a handful of scientists and technicians reporting to me, and difficulties arose between two of them. Joan Brody, a recent hire with a no-nonsense view of life, started having communications issues with Jeremy Hill, the scientist guiding her first steps in materials composition research. Though he was responsible for her work, Jeremy was not perceived by Joan as being straightforward with data, keeping valuable insights and crucial results from her. Time would prove this not to be the only time when a woman scientist would find in Jeremy an unwilling collaborator, but at that moment a pattern had not developed.

I worked hard at bringing both Joan and Jeremy to the table so they could identify the behaviors that created difficulties, propose solutions, and reach compromises. We would go through these working sessions periodically, but Joan expressed frustration as she experienced little change in Jeremy's behavior. Jeremy, on the other hand, had little complaining to do or frustration to express. But neither did he express any desire to pursue an understanding of how his behavior affected others.

We marched along, working on strengthening Joan's understanding of materials to the point that she could walk independently from him, but also keeping close tabs on the data and information flowing from him to her to overcome the effectiveness of Jeremy's blocking. It was difficult in these early stages to unravel the conditioning behind his blocking behavior, and Jeremy's lack of interest in developing an awareness of self did not help. Was it a personality conflict, a tendency to protect turf and get in the way of those he saw as intruding, or something else? So to address the behavior and neutralize the universal effect of blockers who get in the way, we worked on developing her capacity to deal with this type of colleague, an important tool that would serve her well into her future.

For decades, Corning as a corporation has made significant efforts and achieved results in understanding and addressing diversity issues, whether of gender, ethnic, cultural origins, or, more recently, sexual orientation. I had been active on the diversity front since its inception in the early 1980s and had provided leadership for the creation of advocacy groups for women, ethnic minorities, and gay employees. Corning occupies a leading position in corporate America on diversity, has a strong corporate culture of diversity, and pursues solutions to issues on a daily basis. But identifying and addressing a conditioned tendency to be dismissive of members of a minority group, a tendency that expresses itself in subtle ways, requires not only keen insight and solid evidence, but also deep commitment on all parts. And resolution takes a long and sustained exploration into self-awareness, which is not effective if forced.

Over the following years, however, a pattern started to emerge. After Jeremy's transfer from research to the development group, his female colleagues would come to me—as the most senior woman in the technology group—for advice on how to handle his unenthusiastic reception of their results and, hence, their difficulty in advancing their findings along the innovation path, particularly when he was on the receiving end. Because no men brought up the blocking behavior that the women were experiencing, the pattern appeared clear to me. But despite Corning's sophistication in dealing with diversity issues, I found no echo in his organization to address the situation. The women who over time had experienced his blocking behaviors moved on to different organizations; the effects of his blocking, though preventing them from spreading their wings and being as effective as they could, were hard to record as devastating to their lives and careers; and, short of commencing a gargantuan detective operation, documenting the pattern would fail. These subtle issues are the most insidious and difficult to address and the most frustrating to a leader. With every new case of the handful that came to me, I could sense the exasperation, the sense of defeat rising in my heart. Furthermore, Jeremy had little inclination to pursue an inquiry into self-awareness, to find out how he was perceived, how his conditioning predisposed his actions, and how his actions affected others. Unable to influence his managers and leaders to join me in pursuing the resolution of Jeremy's issues—which had become apparent only with the perspective of time as the pattern emerged—and unable to influence him informally, I worked repeatedly with these women on bolstering their ability to push through on their own, helping them become familiar with the process of inquiry and connecting to their inner drive to find their source of strength. "We cannot sanitize the world of personalities that we find difficult," I would remind them. "The only one we can change is ourselves." And so they learned about themselves, about finding courage and expressing it as assertiveness. But we also worked on learning to read team dynamics, on creating networks of support, and hence on being able to disarm disabling tactics whether or not they are addressed preferentially to a specific group. So over time, for all of us, the sense that you cannot win them all was paired by a sense that you can learn to thrive in spite of circumstances.

DEFINE ROLES CLEARLY AND INHIBIT CONFLICT

Fervent personalities, driven by willful egos, can grow with time and experience to become overpowering leaders that create intimidating domains, intimidating not just to members of their groups, but to peer leaders alike, for whom it may be easier to stay on the sidelines. But staying—or managing—from the sidelines creates a drag that slows down and sometimes prevents results. Grabbing the bull by the horns may not be effortless or painless, but it is necessary to clear obstructions to the flow needed to deliver results. And just as important as understanding passions and managing personalities is defining roles that are clear to each and all team members, roles that are understood and respected by all but that may be reviewed and refined as projects evolve.

Of Titans and Roles
The Impact of Defining Who Does What

One of my early assignments as I first became a manager of the glass research group in the mid-1990s was to oversee the delivery of new powdered glass compositions into the TV glass manufacturing plants, where they were required for sealing purposes. These were the days prior to LCD technology, when the dominant display technology was CRT-based, and Corning enjoyed a large share of the market, just as it does today with precision glass panels for LCD-based displays. As these bulky sets became larger in size and more sophisticated in features, Corning led the way in changing the glass compositions to deliver increased performance, which required changes to the powdered glasses used for sealing the front panel—the screen—to the back funnel that housed the CRT tube responsible for generating the image. For years, Corning, like most glass suppliers, had relied on an outside manufacturer to supply the sealing glass. The research organization identified an emerging need and an opportunity to jump ahead of the game, and it was prompt in creating a project to address it. The business, though, was not as certain of the operating premise, and the initiative lacked uniform commercial support.

Prior to my arrival the glass research group had been investigating powdered glasses for sealing glass to glass and glass to metal, a traditionally difficult bond to make reliably with common adhesives. For several years Rick Laredo, the scientist-farmer, had devoted most of his time to developing the fundamental understanding required to take a practical field and elevate it to a science where systematic principles emerge and can be used for predictive purposes in developing compositions with specific performance requirements. In a few years, Rick, a rigorous and focused scientist, honest to a fault, and with a wry sense of humor who did not suffer fools lightly, would single-handedly develop a technology in powdered glasses for sealing that could give Corning an advantage in applications ranging from lighting and materials to display and future photonics. Within the glass research group Rick's honesty was much appreciated by his colleagues, who could counter his sense of humor and obstinacy with their own. But he found a match who was not keen to humor his ways in Greg Fitzgerald, the director of development responsible for the transfer of the sealing technology from research to the TV manufacturing plants and ultimately to the customers.

Larger than life, Greg Fitzgerald was a powerful personality with an equally imposing physical frame. With a baritone voice that he could use just as impressively in group settings as in his church choir, he knew clearly what he wanted and how to get there. With a data-driven inquisitive mind, by the mid-1990s he had established himself as one of the movers within the technology community, with a solid record of technology delivery across many commercial units and a firm position within the laboratory and the commercial communities. He never hesitated to make his opinion known on his own venue and, when asked, on other projects flowing out of the lab. And, of course, he did not yield to others unless their arguments were substantiated by data: "Stick with the numbers," he would admonish. "It removes emotion." Though he might have appeared hard-nosed, he embodied the respectful manager, never competing with his people, but instead ensuring they got the credit they deserved. Not surprisingly, those in his group loved his willingness to go to bat for them and his success at defending their cause. But most of the technology community treaded lightly around him. It was just not pleasant to be steamrolled by Greg's arguments—particularly in absence of supporting data.

I was a junior manager at that time. I had been brought into the technology community to manage the glass research group after three years of commercial experience in the Consumer Products division. There was a strong historic tie between glass research and the Consumer Products division, as this was the business unit that for years had commercialized many of the new materials invented by Corning scientists and that was largely responsible for the incredibly high brand recognition that Corning enjoyed: polls in those years showed that a full 98 percent of the U.S. population was familiar with brand names such as CorningWare® and Pyrex®. For me, as marketing manager responsible for CorningWare, the whole experience of consumer research, product definition, positioning, advertising, and launching a new product line had been more than just the intended broadening experience; it had been an exhilarating one. So I was charged with energy and a sense of empowerment as I came back into the technology community. I had left as a glass researcher and now I was returning to take responsibility for a group I respected deeply. This sense of empowerment was not diminished in any way by my relationship with my boss, Donald Jameson, the manager who brought me in to take over for him in leading the glass research group. But the request to manage the Rick-Greg relationship still felt daunting.

Donald and I had complementary personalities and forged a strong relationship that lasted for years. Donald gave me the freedom and space to create my own style of leadership. He was supportive of my initiatives without hindering my uniquely different way of doing things, and I was mindful of his own sense of comfort and his strong technology guidance. An astoundingly bright intellect with an exquisite ability to stay on top of every single technology detail and advancement, his skills and interests ranged from classical piano and guitar playing to carpentry and car rebuilding. We shared a passion for delivering technology, and he gave me space in my deep concern for the people involved in its creation and delivery. And I brought in the emotional intelligence part of the equation, the personal touch with the people, and the willingness to jump into the fray. So it was no surprise to me when he asked me to handle the research-development impasse.

Greg was the second development director to be responsible for Rick's project, and this put pressure on the technology transfer from research to development. Donald had been aware of this situation and worried about the lack of communication between the two organizations and his perception that the pace of the project did not match the opportunity sensed by research, and he had attempted to manage it lightly through regular meetings with Greg. As a junior manager asked to look into it more deeply and to get to the gist of things, I found the request imposing: it had all the markings of a clash of giants, with forceful personalities unused to backing out of rows, facing each other from different hierarchical positions.

It was clear to me that I had come back to manage a group of scientists for whom I had a great deal of respect, a group amidst whom I had grown up as an industrial researcher. I was moving from being their peer to being their leader. And it was just as clear in my heart that I needed to gain their respect without compromising on my primary responsibility, which was to create inventions and deliver new technology from them. So I went into uncharted waters with the guidance of my intuition: I opened a dialogue with Greg and one with Rick. I met with them regularly, getting to know them as human beings, understanding their drives, exploring their issues.

I did indeed find a clash of strong personalities, though each of them was open to dialogue with me on their own. But I also found a great lack of structural organization and, significantly, a mismatch in organizational objectives. Today, with the perspective of nearly twenty years of experience in managing and delivering technology, it is easy to say that the issues I encountered are perennial ones in technology transfer, the issues that define the creative tension inherent to two groups with very different objectives and underlying principles but with one common goal: technology delivery.

- Greg, aware of and responsive to commercial demands, promised the customers results and samples that imposed timelines that Rick felt were impossible to meet. "Inventions cannot be scheduled," Rick would respond, adding,

"He thinks that nine women can have a baby in one month."

- Rick, experienced in representing Corning to customers and capable of juggling the demands of simultaneous projects, found the number of project and commercial meetings demanded by Greg to be excessive, cutting back on his ability to do science.

- Greg, with the technical background that is seen as an asset in technology managers and in his relentless pursuit of data in his decision making, had a tendency to provide technical suggestions to the projects, including experiments and composition changes. And he did not hesitate to fulfill his responsibility of making the final decision on the functionality of glass compositions recommended to the commercial group.

- For Rick, a researcher with scientific rigor and cognizant of the demands imposed by a manufacturing environment, the areas in which Greg was acting were the purview of research. In his view, failure to see this was only to be taken as a lack of respect.

- Rick shared the excitement that came from the research organization: the opportunity to develop a new sealing glass technology base for Corning.

- Greg, fully aware of the position of this new opportunity as a small one within the commercial strategy, gave it the more balanced support that business imperatives demanded.

As I saw it, the issue went beyond a need for better communication between two driven, strong-willed personalities committed to deliver on their responsibility. It spilled into something that in time became for me a major pillar of managing creativity to deliver results: strategic alignment and role definition, discussed further in the context of the need for clear organization structures.

The relationship between the business unit and the customer is the role of the commercial manager, so in an attempt to understand their business strategy, I served as the link to the marketing director of the division, invested the time in creating a relationship with him, and asked him to play a stronger role in the project. Unlike the other personalities, this was an easy relationship and, for me, represented an oasis in this otherwise highly strung cast of characters. There was also a need for a project manager, who is the person responsible for defining timelines and commitments and for honoring and understanding the needs of his two constituencies: researchers and receivers. This took a bit of doing because the project, though part of the business unit strategy, was a small one and could not take on a large team. This would be the first of two situations when I would find myself in the less-than-desirable double role of playing the single project manager while simultaneously being the functional manager for the group. I had already established a constructive relationship with both Rick and Greg, so working with each of them to give the other more flexibility and slack was a rewarding first experience in managing creative tension.

There were indeed differences in personalities, in styles, and in perspectives between Rick and Greg, but the core of the issue was a disparity in strategic objectives. Rick's drive obeyed the research imperative of opening a new area of technology for the corporation, that of sealing glasses, that might develop into a broad area, serving many business opportunities. This is the purview and responsibility of research. Greg's perspective, on the other hand, reflected business imperatives: the sealing glass business was undergoing changes throughout the world, and as the business unit looked at the forecasted changes, they were not as certain of the operating premise. This drove the lack of uniform commercial support for the initiative. And for projects to move on to deliver inventions and advances into applications, the alignment of the two—the new technology coming from research and the business need and opportunity—is an imperative.

So the effort needed to address this case was not just the establishment of a relationship of dialogue between two players, but the understanding of the business imperatives within the research organization. It was the steady, diplomatic but firm work of realigning two organizations so their tracks could run smoothly. With time, tensions eased off, communication improved, strategies were understood and internalized, project objectives could be reviewed in a spirit of trust, decisions were made that relied on data, and Greg and Rick worked together, respecting each other and their views. Greg saw the project path following business imperatives, and other applications were pursued where the sealing technology had greater commercial impact.

The urgency of goals and the numbers of players may vary, compounding the issues, but the fundamental human issues that stifle creativity and drive are common to teams fueled by powerful personalities and chasing ambitious delivery targets. With the aggressive growth objectives of organizations today, the increased complexity of major innovations, and the temptation of upper leadership to become hands-on managers of high priority projects, there is an increased risk of freedom being overpowered by control. Today, more than ever, breakthrough delivery requires the creation of organizational structures that will balance respect and urgency and, in doing so, eliminate the barriers created by multiple, unbalanced roles and demands.

Finding My Wings

CAREER at Corning, as I started broadening my cir-
ger—though certainly not large—numbers of women
chnology group, I could tell that I did not *quite*
belong. Corning was my first corporate experience and never in
any of my previous academic and research endeavors—from the
Universidad Nacional de Colombia at Medellín, to Stanford University in California, to the Carnegie Institution of Washington, to
the Max Planck Institüt in Germany—had I experienced this feeling. I was finding a group of very smart women, who appeared
very poised and who were able to express their opinions in a
reserved, almost demure, way. Their views were not hidden, but
they were never intrepid either. Their attire was always well coiffed
and polished, you could say even conservative. The style in those
days of the early 1980s was dictated by "dress for success"
canons, which had proven successful in delivering the right message: I am here and I will make it.

As I got to know these women leaders of the corporation—
the ones from whose ranks emerged the high-ranking leaders of

today after the substantial attrition typical of women trying to break the glass ceiling in American corporations—I learned to admire them, to enjoy them, to seek their advice, and to befriend them. Some of them are to this day my best friends. In those days, though, I could not help but feel that I did not quite fit in. Not that I was not given space or that my opinions were not received. To the contrary, I was sought out to participate in problem-resolution corporate teams and bring in a fresh viewpoint, as I was developing a reputation for speaking my mind—a *unique* reputation, as it turned out. My delivery style, energized, even agitated, and supported by hand gesturing—one that was matter-of-fact in the Latin culture from which I emerged—felt oddly out of place. My zest for bright colors—emerald greens and purples, bright reds, oranges, and pinks—and my own unique designs in clothing, though often admired, stood out amidst the sea of dress-for-success pinstriped grays and blacks. And I would find later through HR feedback that my courage in speaking my mind was not necessarily scoring me points in career advancement.

I felt that bringing my real self into the workplace could jeopardize my career—could such a different woman represent the corporate interests of the conservative culture that Corning stood for? But the feeling that not bringing my whole self in, that putting on a professional face that was not my own would suffocate me, was stronger. I did not have a coach or a supervisor to guide me along, a sounding board that, with my best interest at heart, could help me sort things out. In looking back it is clear that what I needed then was the encouragement and support to bring my whole self in and the guidance to make it a success. But this was my own path to plow. So, in an unperceptive way, I stayed true to myself and followed my heart. In my external self I continued to enjoy my textiles, colors, and designs. In my internal process I started to learn about detachment and space. I observed others and listened, learned to reflect and hold back, made an effort to understand my effect on others—a process of becoming "Anglicized," as I would call it. One step at a time, unknowingly, I was learning about the building blocks of awareness of self and putting them into practice. It would be years before I would encounter Dasa, who accelerated my learning.

Perhaps it was my *uniqueness* that colored the choice made by the director of research at the time as he selected the manager to succeed Donald Jameson as manager for glass research. As the only supervisor in the group, I was the expected successor. Instead, the research director chose a well-intentioned and bright scientist, but by not understanding the skills and strengths of the person he chose and following the common belief that the best researcher makes the best functional manager, he chose one who did not, as his career would later show, have the vision or people-management skills that high-powered, independent, and sarcastic scientists need from their leader. It was a painful first experience of being passed over for promotion. Worse yet, under the new manager, the group felt demoralized. After a few months, I needed out.

During the previous couple of years, my technical work had delved into materials for the Consumer Products division, which for decades had inspired much research and advancement in materials and had found applications for them in new products. It was so much a part of Corning's culture that the sale of the consumer products business later in 1998 was emotionally difficult for the entire corporation. As a result of my inventions I had developed a good relationship with Raymond Hurley, the senior vice president of sales and marketing for the business, an experienced man with broad-ranging knowledge of and an instinct for consumer markets. I had visited him regularly to show him the new materials I was inventing in search of his support in developing them into new products. He had gotten to know me, my love of materials and their application, my willingness to challenge odds and barriers, the flamboyancy in my style. And he had been supportive and encouraging. These were the early 1990s, which represented hard times for what had been one of Corning's most successful and longer-lasting businesses; all the brands were under the siege of cheaper imports from the Far East that were precipitating a steady decline in sales.

I approached Raymond in search of an expanding opportunity, and I was astonished when, after some reflection, he offered me the responsibility of rescuing the division's flagship brand, CorningWare, from what felt like an unavoidable fall. He needed somebody who would do things in unconventional ways, who could think independently and take the pressure, and he knew me enough to trust that I could. And I had Donald's endorsement. Not knowing whether I had just won the lotto or signed my own death warrant, I took on the charge of product line manager without having as much as a short course in marketing. But Raymond had seen something in me and was willing to trust me, and when I asked him where I could find training, he exclaimed, "On the job! This will be baptism by fire." Unsure of myself, I trusted that he would remain right behind me as my compass needle. And he did, adding decades later, "You underestimate how much confidence I had in you."

From the beginning, I enjoyed the support of my colleagues, who were a fun and invigorating community of professionals steeped in the art of marketing and responsible for the Corning brands and for developing new products, though early on they were as puzzled as I was as to why I had been given the job. It was an exhilarating experience, and I could not get enough of it. Carrying out consumer research, leading focus groups, arriving at a product definition, creating product positioning and consumer segmentation, was just the beginning of my exploration of this new world. As a result, we identified an opportunity to go through the revival of the classic CorningWare brand, updated for the lifestyle of a new consumer and presented as Casual Elegance: Cookware that Serves.

I found myself immersed not only in the technical development of a new glass composition with a warmer shade of substrate color, which was second nature for me, but in the new world of advertising and PR, which I found fascinating and where I enjoyed developing print ad campaigns, planning events, and shooting TV commercials. The project team I was leading was under significant pressure because of the dire financial condition of the division and the need to shore up sales with a new product. What ensued was the division's fastest-paced project in more than twenty years, going from product concept to sales launch in eleven months. Experience has shown us all that if not managed, a fast-paced project brings out the worst tendencies in team members. And so, in the commercial setting, I faced my first experience in understanding human drive, in creating alliances, managing conflict, capturing the best that each player had to offer, inspiring, and leading. By the end of three years, we had achieved 100 percent distribution on existing accounts and expansion to new key accounts, resulting in a 12 percent increase in sales and an 82 percent increase in contributing operating margin.

Overjoyed by the stimulating experiences and convinced that I had found my calling in the commercial world, I first ignored Donald Jameson's call to join him back at the technology group to manage the glass research group. I was not aware that my life path was about to turn and that I had already started to put together the various experiences that would coalesce into my passion and understanding of the creative human drive.

Let the Best Take Flight

THE FIRST STEP in building a high-performance team is to get passionate, brilliant, and creative people in the room, and to do so you need to look with eyes that are as rich as their lives. Beyond stellar academic or work credentials, it is essential to get a sense of the candidate's fit with your organization by looking for the person—her upbringing and personality, ability to see wide-open spaces balanced by the need to remain highly focused, life at home and in the community, and reactions to those circumstances. Just as crucial is the need to look outside the person's work life for expressions of creativity, such as hobbies, activities, and a zest for life.

NOT ALL THE PASSIONATE ARE CREATED EQUAL

It is easy to oversimplify and label practitioners in a field as sharing traits and even personalities. Perhaps the most widely accepted stereotype is that of scientists and engineers as "nerds." When people think of scientists, they often see them as "left-brain" people: logical, sequential, rational, analytical, and objective. When you take the time to know them, however, you see it differently. Some of the most successful people in scientific, technical, or engineering fields also make room for "right-brain" traits: intuitive, holistic, random, synthesizing, and subjective. They follow their hearts. And such is the case for practitioners in *any* field. The "impassioned" show a vibrancy in their personal lives and, often, multidimensionality in skills and interests, from music to woodworking, rock climbing to weaving. And when you bring them together, these interests and skills will inform the reactions between players and their collaborations and create the persona of the group.

Spotting Creatives
Be Prepared to Be Surprised

Some of the most successfully creative technical people I have led and worked with are musically talented and accomplished. I can think of talented classical piano players such as Peter Murray, geologist turned glass scientist, who sings with a tenor voice and also enjoys cooking ethnic foods. Jacques Montebourg, a physical chemist who later demonstrated people-managing and leadership skills and could turn an unenthused group into a motivated one, is a skilled clarinet player good enough to have joined a philharmonic orchestra, and who played delightful duos with Jeannie Brown, an electrochemist with a broad and fertile palette of textile art techniques under her belt, on the flute.

For some scientists, their kitchen becomes their personal

chemistry lab and a liberating—and tasty—way of being creative. Dave Johnson is a geologist with a superb ability to take the most basic and fundamental principles of science and use them to model a system and predict the conditions that would solve an issue, whether dealing with material properties or manufacturing glitches. Outside the lab setting, he enjoys taking his love of food into an exploratory realm, varying recipes, testing, tasting, and inventing, to come up with the most exquisite smoked and grilled meats, always accompanied by delightful side dishes prepared with his wife Betty, a talented painter, sculptor, and garden landscape artist. Over time, these gourmet meals became an important element of the social bond of the glass research group.

Joe Fishlinger, a polymer scientist with an understanding of chemistry and rheology of organic materials, turned his knowledge into high-quality truffle making that rivaled the most prestigious European chocolatiers. Using the best ingredients—Belgian chocolate, Indonesian vanilla, and the like—he would produce golf ball–sized truffles and wander around the lab offering them. His parade along the hallways would prompt all of us to come out of our offices, and he and the lab would benefit from the dialogue that ensued, touching on all subjects. Later on, his passion expanded to growing basil, collecting leaves by the bushel and creating exquisite pesto that he would jar and distribute in his unique truffle-like tradition.

For others, the rigorous nature of their research minds finds outlets in nature. Brian MacHarg, another geologist with an unstoppable drive to explore "esoteric glass research"—as his answering machine proudly announces—has cultivated an interest in butterflies and ferns since childhood. He has amassed a worldwide collection of each and a knowledge that rivals that of Smithsonian Institution curators. Rounding out his life is a passion for sports that found him coaching boys and girls soccer for years and playing hockey in adult leagues.

And then there are the indomitable explorers who in their personal lives echo their passion to go where no other has previously been in their scientific quest. People like Olivier Chauvel, a mechanical engineer with an independent streak and a rebellious attitude from the day he was hired, the same that led him later to ignore conventional wisdom and make significant contributions to extending Corning's ability to form difficult glasses into precision glass. And the same spirit that inspired him to, with no previous blue water sailing experience, single-handedly rebuild a sturdy sailboat that carried him and his wife on a six-month sailing voyage above the Arctic Circle, into the even colder and icier waters of 80-degree northern latitudes.

Occasionally you find those who have multiple talents, like Donald Jameson, a chemist with a Ph.D. from M.I.T. who in addition to playing classical piano since childhood, taught himself as an adult to play folk guitar, enjoyed rebuilding cars, and could turn wood into beautiful pieces of furniture. Or François Sunik, a mechanical engineer who could always come up with an innovative way to process glass into any shape imaginable, from fibers to continuous sheet, to funnels or honeycomb structures. He had interests and broad knowledge in areas ranging from the druid world to Renaissance culture, relished organizing art shows, enjoyed taking long bike and camping trips as much as leading guided weekend community walks, and spent days with his children building unique pieces such as "unsinkable" canoes with his own innovative design and using solar/thermoelectric principles.

Real creativity is productive and its expression yields a constant stream of output: a canoe for the family one month, an improved telescope system the next; a butterfly collection that keeps on growing; a new garment of wearable art every season. These are some of the signs to seek as output for social or family activities, and they are a good predictor of professional output. These are not passing fancies. They are the materialization of a creative flow that is ongoing. So it is important that the hiring process be rich enough to allow you to unearth, explore, and walk around these passions to inform your decision. Some of these interests develop with time, but you can still spot them in a young person.

BUILD FROM RELATIONSHIPS AND HIRE WITH HEART

I believe in the richness of a recruiting process that puts value in personal relationships rather than one that can put a taller stack of resumes, assembled by an external firm, on your desk. It is this process that enables the creation of vibrant groups with the ability to innovate and to turn cutting-edge inventions into real products. This, of course, needs to be a rigorous process, one with well-defined statements that are circulated among the participants and serve as a guide for discussions and decisions: purpose of the position, major responsibilities, activities, and links. Once you have built a core team and a culture of inclusion, impassioned practitioners will be able to engage in relationship-based recruiting, spotting each other as peers and enlarging the high-caliber circle. Team members will have connections to their alma maters and will be active in external professional societies. It is through these personal contacts that one can follow the trail that opens the person, the interests, the excitement.

Hiring offers a rich opportunity for the creation of fertile elements of culture as it presents the leader with situations that call for empowering leadership. In an empowered group, inclusion need not be demanded because it is an intrinsic part of the persona of the group. And nowhere is inclusion as vital in preserving culture and empowerment as in the hiring process. Bring your team members into the complete hiring process, from identifying candidates to sitting around the table for the candidate discussion to participating actively in decision making. Yes, these may traditionally be the purview of the leader and, yes, it may feel that your authority is weakened as your technical leaders express views that oppose yours and disagree on your choice. But not only will the quality of the practitioners selected be optimized and the concordance with the group maximized, but your ability to lead will be enhanced as you practice empowering leadership, listening to the input of the team, encouraging diversity of opinion, being willing to change your view in the light of new perspectives and information.

Recruiting Is a Team Game
Be True to Your Commitment

We had two very strong candidates during the process of hiring a glass scientist that could shore up our glass compositions efforts when Corning decided to expand its flat glass business into new market segments. With a few exceptions in the world, glass science is not an area where universities offer programs or grant degrees. For years, Corning has been used to hiring scientists with Ph.D.s in areas such as material science, chemistry, and geology and, through mentoring by senior researchers, transforming them into well-versed glass researchers who end up being recognized by the international scientific community. This time, however, through our collective informal network, the group had been able to identify two unusual candidates with solid glass experience. Peter Murray, the first one, had more than five years of experience in glass composition at a national lab. Rabbindrana Raja, a postdoctoral fellow in the UK, had gotten a Ph.D. at Stanford University under one of the few geology professors in the world using sophisticated analytical tools and equipment to model glass systems relevant to the geological world.

Their backgrounds were solid, their experience impressive, their publications spoke for themselves. As a group, we all wished we could hire them both. But even for the one opening, we were stretching the budget. The discussion was long and arduous. It was clear to me from everybody's input that Peter had the fiery personality that requires solid and persistent management. Rabbindrana, on the other hand, was a gentle being with the ability to remain centered in the toughest battles—but no weaker professionally for his lack of temper. You could have tossed a coin. In the end, I leaned toward Rabbindrana, whereas the group in no uncertain terms recommended Peter. The choice of Peter was not even a calculated risk, but it did push me, as a leader, to be true to that sense of empowerment that I had espoused all along in our group, whether the actual round-the-table discussion felt comfortable to me or not. And it proved in the short and long terms to enrich our culture and to open repeated doors for Corning.

Rabbindrana, the other candidate, stayed in the back of everybody's mind. He was too good to be forgotten. After a couple of years, as Corning embarked on a phase of hyper-growth to enter the photonics bubble—a venture that ultimately led the corporation to a near-death experience—the glass research group found itself in the situation of not being able to find glass scientists and technicians fast enough to meet the demands of the corporation for new materials for photonic applications. Rabbindrana came to our collective minds immediately. He found his place amidst a group that welcomed and valued him, where he was given the freedom afforded to creative minds, and where he followed the trail dictated by his instincts to find important contributions to make.

In bringing together a truly creative team, leaders need to broadly accept and rejoice in wildly different styles and use them to the advantage of the team or project. Allow the personal styles, strengths, and needs to inform how they will be brought together in dynamic, highly interactive teams. Team members need to be complementary, not only in scientific disciplines but along every dimension of their professional and personal lives. Many of their interests can be drawn out to enhance team dynamics, particularly communication. Just recall the successful intervention of Rick Laredo on team dynamics, achieved thanks to his ability to bridge the communication gap between two key players, Peter Murray from research and Chris Cunningham from development.

When you have developed a system that works, it is tempting to be bound by it. But for leaders as much as for creatives, flexibility is an attitude that prevents damage by repetition. As a leader, you too need to tap into that source of intuitive wisdom and to follow the trail, that inexplicable knowing that you cannot logically explain, that may at times take you through the thorny thicket. If you remain flexible and alert to explore outside the preferred process, you can benefit from random acts, those unexpected events that bring you a solution just when you need it.

Dropped from the Sky
Benefit from Synchronicity

Just prior to the advent of Corning's hectic period of hyper-growth, we saw the need to create a solid level of fluorine chemistry understanding in the glass research group. The objective was to address the needs of the optical fiber business, which in the 1980s and 1990s represented by far the corporation's largest source of income and profit. Most of optical fiber's research up until those days was devoted to process research, and Corning had a nice process advantage in the marketplace as a result of a well-established and rigorous culture of technology innovation that enabled a seamless transfer of technology from research to development to manufacturing. At Corning, fiber research and development was carried out in groups directly tied to the business unit, and the input of the glass research group, a core group servicing all business units, was not considered essential to optical fiber.

But we begged to differ. Knowing the capabilities of the thoroughbred researchers that we had and their ability to invent new materials with properties required in whatever field of application we requested, my boss and I, contrary to public opinion, felt clearly that it was indeed our responsibility to address the needs of the optical fiber business. Hence we began the search for an expert that could buttress our understanding of glass with the knowledge of the chemistry of that tricky element—fluorine—that is key to the processing of glass for optical fiber.

As we were searching and making connections with our network of faculty members and researchers in the fluorine chemistry community, a letter arrived in the mail, addressed directly to me, from Isabel Lopez, a Ph.D. candidate from Berkeley working on fluorine chemistry with one of the leading academic forces in the field. Her only connection to glass was as a budding glass artist in California who, in her search for glass supplies and companies, had been captivated by Corning's breadth and depth of materials research and decided to contact us. A stroke of luck, an example of inspired initiative, or the answer to our prayers? A first phone screening suggested all of the above, and I invited her to come for an interview and to bring along her fiancé, who I found out was a Canadian postdoctoral fellow at Berkeley, also doing fluorine chemistry. We learned that not only could she prop up our glass research with her solid understanding of the field, but she brought a wonderful complementarity to the group in areas that were new to us and refreshing: her flair for design, her interest in yoga and Eastern cultures, her life experience as a Hispanic, and her freshness and transparency. Her fiancé, an exquisite experimentalist in the traditionally difficult field of fluorine chemistry and an accomplished classical and Spanish guitar player, was just the icing on the cake. After the two-day interview, we made them tandem job offers as I drove them to the airport to catch their flight back to California. They drove to Corning to start on their new jobs shortly after their wedding.

In hiring, the toughest of all assignments is to find your own successor. In dry terms, you need to find somebody who can lead and deploy technology resources to create and deliver for today, for tomorrow, and for beyond, somebody who can provide flexibility and interconnectivity for the group, and who can foster creativity for invention and delivery. In spirit, what you need is the guardian of an institution, somebody who can continue the culture and the tradition, not by being a copycat but by ushering in a style of his own, somebody who can be true to himself and who will be respected but not feared by your group. What you are looking for is a true leader, for you arc, after all, about to entrust your cherished treasure to somebody else while giving the successor the space to become a leader in his own right.

A Team Needs a Leader
Finding Your Successor

Being the manager of glass research at Corning had energized me, inspired me, and challenged me in equal proportions. I had taken a group of fifteen scientists and technicians and grown it to more than forty. We had delivered technology jointly for all major divisions of the corporation—display, lighting and materials, consumer products, and, more recently, optical fiber and photonics—created strong ties to business leaders, and gained credibility as the core research group that excelled at serving the diverse needs of Corning's many businesses. The culture was fast-paced and upbeat, the celebrations intimate and festive. As I was assigned larger responsibilities, however, it was imperative to find the next guardian of the great tradition of research that I had led for six years.

We followed the inclusive hiring process that the group had successfully used for its growth, enlisting the more senior and insightful researchers in the group and enlarging it to bring in, of course, the leadership of Corning's science and technology group. We searched high and low, identifying both internal and external candidates. For the scientists, as for me, it was a bittersweet process, one in which we were all heavily invested.

We brought in candidates with substantial research management experience, and candidates with little; people with experience in academic, national, and industrial lab settings; managers responsible for large groups, and entrepreneurs who had only managed small teams. All were strong candidates with solid records. The scientists, with their understanding of the risks of a mediocre outcome, were serious, insightful in their questioning, and, of course, harsh in their criticism. I have always believed in letting their sarcasm—as well as their excitement—come through uncensored, and this was not the moment to be polite. They were looking for the technology and strategic direction skills, indeed, but they were also digging hard for the person with the skills to lead them. In a composite of their comments about those candidates that we did not hire, one can read a deep understanding of what they were looking for in a leader:

- I tried to get some idea of what his vision for glass research would be, but he really didn't answer the question. I also tried to get some impression if he would be a "microman-ager" or not and again was not really satisfied with his answer. It's hard to quantify, but there was just something about him that "was not all there."

- Poor response to dealing with "very difficult persons" despite claims to having dealt with such. No apparent inter-est in what we're working on. I was never asked about what I do—I would have expected at least some curiosity.

- I didn't get the idea that he'd be enough of a visionary to handle a research group.

- He never once asked either of us what we sought in a boss, what our work experience was like, even what kinds of research we perform. I had a very tough time getting a word in edgewise to ask him questions about his vision for glass research.

- He lacks the sensitivity to respond effectively to the wide range of personalities and styles he would encounter as manager. I was apparently not alone in my impressions, and people with styles very different from my own had much the same reaction.

- I was particularly struck by the apparent lack of interest he expressed in the women that he met, as they reported to me. High-performance teams involving both sexes and diverse styles and approaches to research and work life are realities around here. I question whether he could deal with either.

There is no such thing as the perfect candidate, one who has all the experience, the human skills, and the spirit for the job. So it is important to be able to spot the promise, to smell the potential, to envision the growth. The final decision was mine along with the leadership of the technology group, and they were comfortable with my proposal of taking a risk on somebody who had never managed a large group but who had a solid understanding of materials-based technology and a bright intellect—plus a rich tradition of Andean music with his family group who participated in community and other events—somebody who elicited this kind of response from the scientists in the group:

- I was very impressed with his perceptive approach to people management. He spoke from his experience as a scientist, and said that "often managers think that scientists are all the same, but everyone has a life outside of work, some play music, some like to go hiking, etc."

- He talked about work style, saying, "Some people like to work alone, some like to work in groups, some like to lead or follow. You have to know how people work, you can't put the wrong person on a job and expect them to perform."

- He said that if he were offered the position his approach would be to listen to people, learn how things work, and then he could see where and how he could contribute in his role as manager.

- I think he has the sensitivity to be a good people manager, both in terms of reading people and also understanding how to motivate them.

- At one point he was telling us about speaking to you on the phone and said that you seemed to be a very strong woman. He said that his mother and sister had raised his entire family, and he knew that when a woman was in charge, things would get done! No gender bias here, unlike other candidates.

They knew they had found a manager who would respect them and whom they could respect. The management of the lab knew they had found a manager who could understand technology and strategy and in whom they could entrust the legendary glass research group. I knew he could become a leader capable of creating a culture of creativity and delivery. We were all right. Manuel Cáceres, a scientist from Chile with a Ph.D. in materials science from Colorado, had spent three years doing research in glass for the Atomic Energy Commission back in his country before moving to New Jersey, where he was the president and co-owner of an entrepreneurial effort in advanced materials. I invested time in coaching and developing him, and there were rough moments early on when I felt discouraged and doubtful— the challenges of coaching. Time has shown that the risk paid off: today, after years of his leadership, the group maintains its vibrancy, its dose of quirkiness, and its strong delivery. That much is clear as you walk the hallways of the department and hear from the scientists themselves. He has kept the traditions alive and they feel invigorated, motivated, and challenged by his leadership. Manuel is also enriching the lives of the lab and the town as he brings his family group together for concerts of the best of Andean music.

EMBRACE AND FINE-TUNE EVERY PLAYER IN THE ORCHESTRA

Identifying the best and the brightest and successfully hiring those who will resonate with the culture of the group is but the first step. Getting to know the people in your group well enough to support them and to bring their performance—and their impact on the group—to greater heights is where it all begins. Visit them in their offices, talk to them, get to know them as deeply as they are comfortable with, following their leading pace. The discovery of the smart, driven people with engaging personalities, who excel at far-ranging hobbies, the human beings behind the top-level scientists you hired, will enrich your life and stretch your perspectives. Have fun in celebrating their personal idiosyncrasies, in connecting and resonating with their personal passions. But do not keep this knowledge to yourself. Bring the product of these passions to add to the experience of the group and, in doing so, enrich everyone's lives.

Georges Bertrand, a top-level scientist in our French lab, who among other honors had nearly two hundred publications and books to his name, received multiple national medals and awards, and participated in numerous committees at national labs and universities, taught me about the best years for the best wines in France and, in exploring these, about the different cheese regions in the country. This inspired us to enlist a local wine merchant to guide the lab on a wine-tasting night to celebrate reaching a milestone on one of our projects. We were all surprised. For me, the surprise was in finding that this was a new experience on a wide scale in a country of wine connoisseurs; for them, the surprise was that it was indeed a fun, satisfying, and motivating experience.

When I found out that Patrick Godi, a renowned polymer scientist and accomplished guitar player, and Pierre Malliot, one of the managers in the French lab who also enjoyed playing the guitar, had never played together, I invited them both to play together at one of our leadership retreats. I was sure they would find common ground, as musicians always do. What developed was a fun and spirited collaboration that continued to enliven our team-building events and that spilled over to lab-wide celebrations with original songs written for specific occasions. Years had gone by when I received two special presents from Patrick. The first one came in the mail from France shortly after my retirement from Corning was announced: the first CD he had ever recorded and that he wanted to share with me in reminiscence of those inspiring days. It remains one of the nicest presents I have received, for it is, indeed, a piece of himself. The second one, the gift that warmed my heart, came some time later as part of an e-mail. It simply stated, "It was thanks to you that I retook my guitar studies."

For special occasions, such as the promotion of one of the scientists to the top rung of the ladder, I once asked our most accomplished duo, Jeannie Brown on flute and Jacques Montebourg on clarinet, to play at the recognition event. This was received with such applause by scientists, technicians, and administrative personnel that the voice of encore was hard to ignore. For years to come they became the expected performers at those events that demanded that unique special touch.

Music not only soothes and inspires, it helps to channel the intuitive. Edward Ashton brought this understanding of the power of music to its greatest heights. Ned, as everybody warmly knew him, was a senior executive at the office of the CTO with a special touch that allowed him not only to know every employee and his or her issues, but also every project and every demand from the office of the CEO down; he was intuitive enough to even anticipate issues and reactions. He had the pulse of the organization, the solution to every issue, and the tact to handle them. So, when prompted by a group of "music scientists" who had found each other and had been jamming together in somebody's garage, he saw a beautiful opportunity to bring music and its effect on the flow of creative energy to the entire organization. He provided funding for instruments, arranged connections and speakers at one of the large spaces leading to the cafeteria—where by sheer force of habit, the human traffic in search of food would provide an audience—and designated a time for jam sessions. To this day, for an hour and a half on Fridays, lunches are enriched by the sound of drums, electronic pianos, saxophones, guitars, and flutes masterfully played by technicians and scientists who come together to create the notes of improvised jazz and other rhythms that would otherwise remain closeted during the week.

PLAYERS AS COACHES

The opportunities to learn from your people are boundless. About their activities external to work, for sure, but also about the depths and reaches of their understanding. As a leader, whether in technology, architecture, or medicine, you are expected to understand your field, to know where it is headed, and to translate this knowledge into the strategic direction that keeps you ahead of the field. But you will be fooled, and your group and goals poorly served, if you as a leader do not have experts in your group whose knowledge and understanding far exceed your own. And where better to turn for an education than the safety of your own group?

It may feel that you are exposing your ignorance by asking for a tutorial, but not only will it plant you on terra firma from where you can make richer decisions, it will also show respect for the expertise of your people and, furthermore, gain their respect for your awareness and transparency. Sharp intellects are not only keen observers but are also uncompromising in their demands of their leaders. There is nothing more damaging than trying to convey a sense of understanding of knowledge that you lack. If this is new territory for you, give it a try. Enlarging your own experience by learning from them is truly exhilarating for you *and* for them.

Tim Cobb became my tutor as we entered the new field of photonic band gap fiber. He had a Ph.D. from MIT in this precise area, so we had in-house one of the world's experts in this exciting field, one that was both new to Corning and new to me. Tim combined an excitement for his field with an ability to communicate and an eagerness to do so. Sometimes I would drop in with short questions, whereas at other times we would set aside a couple of hours for an in-depth discussion.

I reached out to Dave Johnson for discussions on the effect on the properties of glass as its atomic structure was modified by exposure to moisture, and to Paul Genetti on all things optical, for he is our expert on optical properties of glass. And in doing so, we could also carve out time to talk about the college selection of our children—theirs and mine—the health situation of an aging parent with Alzheimer's, or the next dance recital they were putting together.

Learning from your experts is not only an enriching experience for you as a leader, but it is one of the first elements of sharing knowledge, an important element in creating a persevering culture where creativity thrives and innovation delivers. I discuss it here from the perspective of a role that enlarges the traditional circle of influence of creative practitioners and their relationship with the group leader. But it also has an immense influence in the creation of a group culture, and I discuss that further in the section on creating a culture.

MAKE ROOM FOR INTUITION

Whether musicians, painters, or scientists, creative people are capable of eliciting the inexplicable, of following the scent of an ill-defined "something" even though they may not know why or where it will lead. For the writer or the architect this may be just sitting down to the typewriter—or the computer, a notebook, or a piece of scrap—and letting whatever comes flow onto the paper. They may not know where it comes from, but the creatives know the experience well. Frank Gehry, whose designs turned the world of architecture on its head and whose buildings move experts and laymen alike with emotion, puts it simply as he says: "I don't know," where it all comes from, "I call it a magic trick."

For the scientist it may be finding another approach away from the tried-and-true, searching in an unlikely compositional field, finding a solution to the impossible.

We see this in Brian MacHarg, who for years has single-handedly pursued the understanding of oxygen-free glasses, following a trail that only he seems to be able to sniff and only a handful of people in the world are able to match in understanding. It is not clear to Corning whether this will only create a leadership position in fundamental science and academic interest, or whether, in thirty years, it will find an application. Still now, as he was doing in the late 1990s, he is being allowed to pursue his passion. For Corning has learned that there is value in letting these inspired scientists and leaders in their field pursue inventions with no apparent immediate application. In the 1970s Corning, by resuscitating a nonmelting process for making the highest purity glass, one that had been invented by one of its scientists puttering around forty years earlier and, finding no application, had been properly documented and shelved, was able to jump ahead of the competition with a manufacturing process for optical fiber still unmatched in efficiency, control, and flexibility. Similarly, the process Corning uses today for manufacturing its precision flat glass used today in computers, televisions, and smartphones was archived for many years after proving too expensive for the windshield application for which it was first conceived and invented.

When thinking of scientists, it is easy to envision only their "left-brain" features—logical and sequential thinking, rational and objective approach, analytical method. But this is only part of the picture. In most successful scientists, as in creative practitioners in all fields, you find ample "right-brain" traits—intuitive perception, holistic approach random methods, synthesizing and subjective approach. How else can you explain the success of scientists who pursue intuitive feelings that they cannot logically explain? I call this state "scientist on a roll": when one good result follows another, you see the total picture and make predictions that are then confirmed by your experiments, and you are being pulled by a "force" and all the pieces fit in nicely. As a leader, nothing compares to the experience of seeing scientists taking creative detours from conventional wisdom, aligning concrete knowledge with their senses and feelings, and producing successful outcomes.

> Peter Murray, now a seasoned scientist with solid credentials in delivering glass compositions into manufacturing and in addressing process hiccups, in his characteristic no-holds-barred style clearly expresses the richness of his exploratory research, where he is granted all freedom: "I have my own project, glasses for display. It is the only place where I can do research. Projects are the death of real research. You cannot do innovation when you have already spelled out the achievements before you start."

If nothing else, one thing is common to creative people: as they follow that drive, that intuitive guide, they are fully convinced of its truth. And though the personalities and hence the expressions may change, there is a powerful force propelling the materialization of the idea. For creativity that is not realized is frustrated creativity. Creative people are driven to make real their dreams, hunches, and drives a material reality. And in so doing they are not willing to have any obstacles stand between them and their vision—hence the need to embrace conflict and, by doing so, transmute it into a creative force.

If given the freedom to be, the creatives themselves will guide you in how leadership can best help them—and the organization—to deliver. You will hear them expressing frustration to the pressure that upper management can impose when, in their zeal to accelerate a high-priority project, they put all their efforts and people around a project, not realizing the effects of micromanaging and of flooding the system with people who have to climb a new learning curve. If you create an environment of trust and spend your time listening, you will understand the needs and the frustrations as you hear comments such as:

- I was trying at one point to orchestrate four tank trials at a time. When am I supposed to do new composition work? Never!

- We knew that the glass was not ready to meet customer specs, so we did all those tank trials to please upper management. They said, "We will do them," and all the VPs followed. But we knew the glass would not work, would not meet the minimum targets for the customer.

Wisdom, then, lies in giving researchers true freedom, not just paying lip service to their need for freedom, while at the same time providing enough structure to guide the results of this exploration to safe—and yielding—shores. This sense of freedom will not only be felt by individual creatives, but will be shared through informal means. Recognition of this behavior will then lead to its emulation. As discussed in the context of creating a culture, sharing and emulating are important elements to the development of a culture of innovation.

The role of the leader is to act as shock absorber for the organization, to understand the needs of the commercial group on one hand and, with the knowledge of what it takes to preserve the space needed for invention on the other, to define goals that can benefit both sides. The role of the leader is also to take the beating, the pain, and the stress of the negotiating process away from the creatives.

SUPPORT CREATIVES TO BRING IN ALL THEIR TALENTS

If Van Gogh had even had a glimmer of the impact of his work on the world, there might be many more Van Goghs for sale today. Whether in art, music, or science, appreciation fuels creativity, not just appreciation of the scientific or technical contributions *alone*, but of the human beings behind them. What fosters creativity is the freedom to engage the integral self, the *total being*: the musician in the scientist, the newlywed in the technician. We should not be afraid of moving to free up and channel the energy and the creativity that allows scientists to engage their total being. Enable, encourage, and even cajole them to bring their entire selves to the job.

Creativity will only run on half the cylinders if you ask people to leave the rest of their lives at the door. Invite them to bring all aspects of their lives and personalities into their work life, every day. Get to know your people, understand their lives, open your arms to their quirkiness and uniqueness, and be bold in finding solutions to their needs. Freeing up and channeling the energy and the creativity means different things to different people. The flow of the creative process, just as that of water in streams as they encounter rocks, is prevented by the blockages of tensions and concerns, of fears and rejection. To encourage practitioners to bring their whole self into the workplace and channel all their creative energy, we must know them first.

He Can Dance!
The Liberating Force of Playing with All Your Gifts

In 1995, when I first started managing the glass research group, I got to know Tim Cobb, a brilliant physicist who had pursued a successful eight-year career at Corning doing sophisticated mathematical calculations in almost exclusive collaboration with his guide and mentor, one of Corning's research fellows. The contributions stemming from Tim's calculations were solid, though the work was performed in near isolation, and there was little connection to other personnel, their projects, lives, and issues. In some ways, it was an ideal existence, to be working at the frontiers of physics, math, and materials without any meddling. As I got to know him, I was interested in what other self there was beyond the mathematical being and how that could inform potential collaborations throughout the group.

Through our conversations I found out that, unbeknownst to most of us, Tim and his wife were accomplished ballroom dancers and instructors. It was surprising that this person, friendly but reclusive, could have a hidden life of carefree twirling around a ballroom floor. His surprise was even greater than mine as I encouraged him to share this side of his life with colleagues inside and outside of Corning. I was asking him to bring the exhilaration and the intensity of his dancing to his life at work, rather than putting it in a compartment that got locked every morning as he walked toward the lab. I wanted him to talk about it and, yes, to give us short workshops on swing or foxtrot before one of our group parties so we could all at least try a few newly learned steps. After a period of hesitation, he responded with enthusiasm. Months later I got a deeper view as I saw the beaming smile on his face as he narrated what it felt like to open his talk on photonic crystal fibers at the MIT symposium he had just attended by weaving his experience as a dancer into his thinking about the complex subject. More than enthusiasm, what Tim was experiencing was liberation.

Feeling that he had much to contribute in collaboration with others, I moved him from the fundamental science calculations that he was so comfortable doing in perfect isolation and assigned him to "less challenging" applied multidisciplinary projects. I could see how his ability to move effortlessly on the dance floor could translate into easy relationships with peers, his ability to instruct dance students into mentoring other scientists. He had already undergone a liberating transformation and I felt that given an opportunity, this same energy could be translated into a transforming impact for Corning's business.

In the 1990s, Corning had a flourishing business making highly specialized lenses used by semiconductor makers in their projection systems for making integrated circuits. After years of sending pulses of laser radiation through the lenses, it was found that the glass shrank infinitesimally and its performance degraded. I assigned Tim to help understand and model the behavior and to explain what was happening and how to solve the problem. It was his first exposure to the agitated environment of a team, one working to deliver a product.

Needless to say, he was frightened. In terms of calculations, the modeling was pedestrian compared to his previous work. But what I was asking for would have an enormous impact on his life and his self-image. Yes, he was aware that in terms of impact to Corning, some of these first calculations had a greater effect than all of his previous eight years of quantum mechanical calculations. But he would be moving from being a fundamental scientist to becoming an applied scientist—an important difference in the scientific world—and from a quiet to an agitated project environment, which would impact his daily stress. For me it was the first experience in having a major impact in a person's life. I was comfortable in following my intuition, but mindful and respectful of my role. What guided me then, and from then on, was the thought that the importance lies not in having him follow my opinion but—as Rudolph Steiner would say—in *his* discovering what is right if I *contribute* something toward his finding it.

What Tim discovered was that, for him, the change was a new and rewarding experience. This was the beginning of the expansion of Tim's career. After eight years he now felt, for the first time, complete in bringing his whole self into the workplace. Looking back at this stage after many years he would recall, "What difference has Lina Echeverría made in my life? All the difference in the world. She helped me grow up. She utterly changed my attitude about what it means to contribute to this lab. She was the first manager to encourage me to bring my 'whole self' into the workplace, and not just my mathematical self or my scientific self. I am a dancer outside of work, but in the past I would not engage this part of my personality in the workplace."

After this first success, and faced with a need to understand the manufacturing conditions for precision flat glass, I asked Tim to do similar "trivial" modeling on the LCD glass crash team. He joined the team and once more had a gratifying experience, one that much time later he would reflect on: "With Lina's encouragement, I have opened up my full personality and found it useful in forming additional connections with colleagues. She helped me discover how better to share the fullness of myself in the workplace. Rather than be embarrassed or put off by differences, Lina is excited and energized by them. She sees my other activities as a source of creativity and energy."

Now, years after these first experiences and after many different projects in as many diverse areas of materials, Tim is so much in demand that he has to make efforts to parcel out his time and to fend off requests for his modeling skills. The scientist who cherished working in isolation and devoting his time to fundamental physics without human meddling has found pleasure in using his human skills, his ability to get along, to become a guide and mentor to others, leading study groups, advising younger scientists, and touching many a project. And it is now, after all these years, that my initial sense of accomplishment at helping Tim grow has truly sunk in. Yes, I could see back in the 1990s that I had had an impact on the results delivered and on the direction of a career. And yes, it encouraged me to follow my intuition and touch other lives, which I did. But I could not have foretold the amazing opening-up of Tim's personality nor his enthusiastic embrace of his total experience. And this, for a leader is—yes—priceless!

LET THEM FOLLOW THEIR HEARTS

Situations where decisions are needed and that can change lives abound in the life of a leader. Each one is unique and each one comes with its own challenges and learning. Treating each with respect and giving it your best effort, however, do not guarantee success. But lack of success is not failure. It is merely part of the experience that forges the leader, with the most powerful lessons possibly being about the illusion of power and control.

Defining Her Own Path
You Will Not Inspire Them All

Material sciences and engineering are not fields where women have traditionally represented a majority. Add to that the paucity of women in upper management positions in corporate America and you find a small number of women with sufficient experience to make a difference in leadership positions in industrial research organizations. So I was looking forward to working with one of these unique women as I became responsible for the group where she worked.

Melissa Jones was a fifteen-year veteran with the corporation. An avid swimmer and a mechanical engineer by training, she had broad understanding of many aspects of Corning's technology, and she had experience that spanned research, development, and manufacturing. In style she had a no-nonsense approach to things that allowed her to deliver results and rapidly address problems and meet needs. In addition, she understood well the organization and the need to communicate and to harmonize strategic direction into execution.

She had been given responsibility as functional manager for a small group when she joined my organization, her first step toward fulfillment of her lifelong ambition of managing a large group of people. I had known her for years and was impressed by her ability to make things happen—whether building connections or delivering technical results—but I had never seen in her an interest in the human being or an ability to light its spark. Nevertheless, she needed to prove to herself—and to the organization at large—that her true calling was indeed in leading people, not in leading projects or transferring technology, as was my initial observation. I observed her for months and could see up close a tendency to provide direction; a struggle with the openness to dialogue that was required; a drive for rapid solutions instead of the support for the ideas of others that was called for; and, of course, I could also see a wonderful ability to respond rapidly to address problems and meet needs.

The feedback from her group was clear: They wanted their input to be taken into consideration, whether regarding a technical matter or their own careers. And what they were getting instead was a tendency to react before listening, a demeanor of certainty, and an overall low level of emotional intelligence. We worked well together; she was an active participant in staff meetings, providing input, supporting initiatives, bringing her own, and always willing to do her part. It was not that her group was performing poorly; projects were delivering results, documentation was on track. It was more that the vibrancy, the inspiration, the passion, were missing. And knowing what she had to offer, I wanted her to do more than good, or very good. I wanted to see her develop to her fullest, to see her shine, to see the energy come through the way it does when skills are aligned with responsibilities, when vocation and avocation meet. I offered her my insight and opened for her a couple of opportunities in technology delivery and transfer where her ability to understand complex technology, to organize, to coordinate and deliver, would allow her to blossom. But I was never able to inspire in her the confidence to trust me enough to change her dream or to create a vision that was vivid enough to be inspiring. I could get her to follow my directives, but I could not win over her heart.

THE GOLDEN RULE: GET TO KNOW THEM, GET TO KNOW THEM, GET TO KNOW THEM

The discovery that beyond the technical or artistic aptitude, there are skills that can be brought to the workplace that allow a person to emerge from the professional cocoon is cause for celebration. For a creative being to find out not only that personality matters a lot, but that her previously hidden ability to communicate with others, to create links between actors, to mentor younger players, is a valuable element in the social process of creation and delivery is a life changer. And this is the central tenet of managing creative people: to tap their talent, to develop new skills, to broaden their experience. In short, to enrich lives.

No group understands better the impact of not being able to bring the whole self into the workplace better than the gay community. Even today, as the world changes and attitudes move, they participate in the workplace as members of a largely invisible, marginalized minority for whom it is generally safest to steer work conversations away from personal life. The penalty, of course, is a fragmented life that rarely allows for easy flow of creativity. For the gay community, bringing one's whole self to work is not so easily done, as even talking about their personal lives can be a source of stress.

Getting to Know You, Getting to Know What to Say

Be Eager to Be Enlightened

I learned this a little bit at a time, starting in early 2000 when Kirsten Steinmeier, a strong person with a quiet demeanor and a degree in electrical engineering, transferred into my group.

Though she was obviously a woman, I was not certain of her gender orientation, nor was I then as knowledgeable about gay issues as I am now, but I knew well that getting to know her was a necessary condition for effective leadership. During our one-on-one conversations I tried to be tactful in asking questions, giving her the space to answer or to avoid them. For me, she was no exception: I was genuinely interested in her and open to her answers. She took the time she needed to come out to me, and only then could I begin the process of really getting to know her. It was an easy, natural process, described best in her own words: "When Lina became my boss, she showed true interest in getting to know me. She asked open-ended questions and was willing to accept whatever I offered in response—even a deflection. Over time I came to trust her and could talk about my life outside of work, including the fact that I was lesbian and had a female partner."

And then my education started in earnest, with Kirsten leading me through what the experience of living in the closet feels like, its effects on her energy, the draining efforts of trying to hide your life from a community whose level of support you have yet to ascertain, the pain of maintaining a compartmentalized life. After knowing that she had a partner, I encouraged Kirsten to bring her to corporate and department events to which spouses were invited. But it was necessary to go further, to give her the space to flourish unencumbered, the support and protection for her to come out of the closet at her pace and in the right moment. Small-town life can be difficult for the gay community, and when you are in the business of delivering state-of-the-art technology you cannot afford to lose the best. I inquired about their adjustment to small-town life in Corning, their joys and concerns, their need for support. Health insurance for her partner was at the top of Kirsten's needs, and after months of looking for broad solutions, I finally decided it was within my reach and I found in my budget a way to cover the cost of her partner's health insurance for a time before domestic partner benefits were officially adopted as a corporate policy.

These changes allowed Kirsten to come into the lab and focus on her work, to relax rather than stress when, on Monday mornings, the conversation revolved around weekends and family life. The dread of how to respond to the harmless question of how had she spent her weekend—should she mention her partner or just talk casually about "friends"—was gone, and she could just be herself. She could put pictures at her desk and create in her office the supporting, motivating atmosphere that others had been enjoying for years.

By 2001 Corning, following both employee and leadership initiatives, had supported the creation of multiple affinity groups, whose main goal was to understand and remove barriers that hindered the performance and advancement of the members of those communities. These groups addressed issues that specifically affected women, African Americans, and other ethnic minorities, but the GLBT (Kirsten's preferred acronym for gay, lesbian, bisexual, and transgendered) community remained where its members had been—in the closet.

I encouraged Kirsten to create an affinity group to address those issues, though early on the main barrier was that the GLBT community was not comfortable enough yet to come out, so, after I joined the group myself, we would meet in private. After a while, the group gathered enough courage and started what had to be the first step: education of top leadership. Through intimate dinner events we started a practice of having a meeting between four or five GLBT members and one top executive at a time. Following a short presentation with personal testimonials and open and transparent dialogue, the group could, in a setting that felt safe for all, answer all questions, bring clarity and understanding, open doors of opportunity. And, most importantly, educate top leadership.

Accepting and bringing her entire being to work, Kirsten took the courageous step of becoming the first visible leader of GLBT issues at Corning, and with her honesty and objectivity led the corporation into the unchartered territories of recognizing domestic partners. Kirsten gained in confidence and assertiveness and, at a professional level, established herself as the corporate expert in thermochemistry, one consulted by the optical fiber, advanced materials, display, and specialty business units. She flourished and grew, bringing forth her respect for the scientific method, her objectivity, and her unquestionable integrity to all exchanges—her own personal guarantee that one can always trust her and her views and recommendations.

Once again the impact of following my instinct was much more strongly felt as time went by. I was satisfied back then with the effort, relieved that things were working out for all and experiencing a sense of accomplishment. With time these feelings did not fade away. They were, rather, joined later by a sense of wonder and appreciation for the trust that Kirsten had placed in my guidance. It was then that I came to realize the feeling of release she had experienced, as she, in the exactness that characterizes her, described it: "Being out to someone is always liberating, but being out to Lina was also empowering. Knowing that this strong-willed, powerful woman was on my side made it possible for me to be a little bolder, a little braver at work. Over time I became both a public face and voice for GLBT employees at Corning— something that would have taken much longer, or maybe never happened at all, without the support of a leader like Lina."

The GLBT group today is a community that participates fully, and with the entire energy of all its members, in Corning's activities, not just in the diversity arena but in all activities of commercial, staff, and technology units. Kirsten continues to flourish as one of the leading forces in educating the community and corporation through conferences, exhibits, documentary films, and, needless to say, their very own presence as productive participants.

FULFILL THEIR EXPANSION OR RISK LOSING THEM

Hiring, expanding, retaining. One could say that the first one is the easy step, the second one is a must, the latter is the crucial one. In creating a culture of expansion, respect, and freedom—to create, to deliver, to be—it is important to understand that the ultimate expression of freedom is the ability to follow your dreams. If an organization does not have the space for your more daring members to spread their wings, their flight will take them away from you. Encouraging people to be their best, providing the support for them to reach greater heights, is a necessary but not sufficient condition for fulfillment. The true test comes when the inner drive of a high performer points in a direction of expansion that collides with your plans, whether they are your strategic plans or your growth plans for the individual. This calls for creative leadership. It calls for the creation of opportunities that encourage spreading our wings and contributions rather than drawing spirits and participation inward.

Closing doors and preventing the creatives from taking flight in an attempt to retain them only creates disgruntlement and fosters discontent, not the energy that a high-performance team feeds on. I am not advocating that we, as leaders, encourage our people—the same people whose quirks and drives we have gotten to know and in whom we have invested our energy and zest to develop and grow—to leave. Maintaining an inspired and motivated state for highly creative, talented individuals is the challenge of leadership. As leaders we need to create cultures that grant our people the freedom to stay. Cultures where leaders exhibit flexibility in responding to needs and identifying opportunities, in creating unorthodox career paths and letting people move outside their groups, in following their people's leads and opening spaces that create opportunities. Cultures of expansion and growth that respond to the needs of individuals and entice them to choose to stay, though they know that their arena is the world and that they are among the best of the world and could go wherever they choose.

On to Other Galaxies
Your Stars May Run Away

Isabel Lopez was a star on track to greater heights. For ten years we had seen her strong technical contributions and her range. Early on we saw her understanding the effect of combustion fuel on transmission losses for optical fiber and recommending the manufacturing conditions that lowered such losses. Soon thereafter, it was developing and transferring to the manufacturing plant a new glass composition for display. And later on, we watched as she demonstrated her ability to inspire and motivate people just as well as she could manage a project—making her the only person I have ever seen excel at all three areas, technical contributor as well as functional *and* project manager. And then we lost her. In her last two years at Corning, Isabel had expanded her concern for energy and the environment into her professional activities, developing a strategy to manage the risks and seize the new business opportunities posed by these global challenges. As a result of her proposal, the group chartered with exploring new technologies and markets was given the mission of finding new opportunities in energy and environmental technologies for Corning, and Isabel requested that she be allowed to participate in this initiative. In an effort to keep this high-potential woman within the technology community, she was moved from research and assigned to the new technologies and markets group.

Despite their best efforts in supporting Isabel by allowing her to pursue a well-known and certified masters program in sustainability, her new group did not have the flexibility in strategic direction or culture that she needed to fly, either to fly and expand herself or to fly and provide leadership in an area that would soon prove to be de rigueur for corporations. For her group leader, Isabel's having educational experience in energy sustainability was one thing—it would provide a useful background—but she was required to get back to the grindstone of evaluating other technologies. Having enjoyed the expansion and growth through her contributions during the previous ten years at Corning, and cognizant of the value she had delivered for the corporation, she felt boxed in, and she struggled with this new sense of constriction. She traveled to France, where I was then running the European technology operations for Corning, to consult me. And I could only continue to be true to my heart in advising her to follow her own.

She was not the only one, she was not the first one, nor will she be the last one to leave. Under similar circumstances, after making his mark by having the inspiration and the guts to open the door to lowering transmission losses of fiber to a historically unthinkable level, Rabbindrana Raja left the glass research group. It happened during a period of uncertainty following a leadership change, when he felt there would be little support for free spirits like himself who were driven by the quest for fundamental understanding. Four years later, the departure of Peter Merkel, who left Corning's European center under uncannily similar circumstances, echoed Rabbindrana's exit. Today they are both professors with thriving research careers at academic institutions, one on each side of the Atlantic. They have kept alive healthy relationships with researchers in the glass research group with similar interests, collaborating in experimentation and theory, participating in scientific conferences, and coauthoring publications.

As a leader who has invested herself in helping each and every one of the members of her group thrive, it is a painful personal experience for me to see them depart, whether or not I still have responsibility for the group. But setting your people free is part of your mission: to prod them, to cajole them, to stretch them so they can grow wings that will then lead them to new places. Whether it is a change in role within the same group, from technical to project management or supervisory responsibilities, or a broadening transfer within the same company looking at markets or business aspects, this is your role as a leader: to grow and liberate, rather than develop and chain.

The departure of one of your superstars does not translate into a loss of vibrancy. The vitality of an organization, that energy that is understood, shared, and amplified by each one of its members, is self-sustaining. Incoming new members, with fresh ideas and spirit, will experience the same guidance and cajoling, not just from the leader, but from all members of the group. And the tradition will live on.

Standing Up for Values

I HAD ARRIVED at Stanford with as much understanding of the advisor–grad student relationship as a foreign student can have. That is to say, hardly any. I had no previous experience or knowledge that could have shaped my expectations. I had been assigned an advisor as an incoming student, and as far as I was concerned, that was all there was to it.

Prior to leaving Colombia for what I thought would be the requisite two years needed to complete a masters program, I had been asked by my alma mater, the Universidad Nacional de Colombia at Medellín, to help them with the organization of an international symposium on ophiolites—rocks that were formed as oceanic crust but that, through continent-building tectonic processes, had been thrust onto the mountains where they are found today. It was not that I had any previous experience in organizing scientific conferences. It was rather that there was nobody else at the hosting university to do it. I was at a momentous transition in my life; I had quit my first job after college and had a few months to fill before leaving for Stanford. It would have been impossible to predict how many roles I had actually signed up for, but after single-handedly dealing with hotel reservations, transportation, simultaneous translators, technical programs, lectures, field trips, and the never-ending logistical issues that characterize these events, the symposium turned out to be a big success, and, significantly for me, it gained me the friendship of the keynote speaker, Andy Bateman.

Little did I know then what an influence he and his wife would have in my life, of opening doors and opportunities, of believing in me and providing undying support while raising the bar for decades to come. Andy, one of the scientists leading the charge in the then-current geological revolution of plate tectonics, is a bigger-than-life, fun-loving, enthusiastic, and motivating giant in his field, with a cadre of followers that spans the world. And he happened to work at the U.S. Geological Survey in Menlo Park, right next door to Stanford. So he made sure that I would call on him when I arrived at Stanford. And he made sure to take me to the field and teach me about ophiolites and California geology, and about the conflicts of scientists, and the "psychology of science." And when it came time for me to choose a dissertation topic—after being encouraged by the faculty to change my goal from a masters to a Ph.D. program—he had plenty of suggestions for me to pick from and an offer to be my scientific advisor, an arrangement not uncommon at Stanford. I chose one topic that presented the puzzling problem of interesting rocks that occur where geological knowledge dictates they should not. They were paradoxical rocks, and they would make for good science, I reckoned. The next issue, of course, the perennial one in academic research, was my source of funding.

The advisor I had been first assigned upon arriving was a young, bright, and ambitious new faculty member putting forth his best effort to make his mark on his way to tenure. Aware of Andy's role as my scientific mentor, he continued to function as my required official university advisor, and I kept him informed of all my findings. It worked for him, particularly when, in my need for financial support, he saw an opportunity to use my thesis topic and initial results to write a National Science Foundation (NSF) grant proposal for funding—as principal investigator and without the knowledge or consent of any of the other players involved. It was only through casual conversation with a master's degree student being funded by not-quite-"my" research grant that I found out what was going on.

Stanford enjoys sunny and mild weather nearly year round and the campus boasts beautifully maintained grounds. In the 1970s the geology graduate students used to have lunch on the lawn under a tree in front of the geology corner. Projects and students, field trips and housing needs, were all discussed there. Older students would opine and advise younger ones. This was how my fellow students found out about my situation and the pain and disquiet it brought me. My fellow students, seasoned Americans who understood well the student-advisor-university relationship, all chimed in in near unison: "Do not make a big deal. You will lose your funding, and that will be the end of your Ph.D. dream." But I was not even being funded by the grant! Then: "Who in the university is going to side with you?" And: "Just make sure that he funds you, and move on." These were the voices of experience talking, but no, this was not what I stood for. Where was my courage?

These were the days before cell phones and e-mail, with international calling rates so high that foreign graduate students like myself would only hear the voices of those back home on special occasions. I had called my older sister on the eve of her wedding, and we were both moved even though we spoke hurriedly, but calling to muse over an internal struggle was not even considered. I knew it all along: This was a situation I would have to face and resolve on my own.

Of six siblings, I had always been the closest to my father, with whom I shared an education as an engineer at the rigorous School of Mines in Medellín, whose board of deans, strangely now but perhaps not atypical during the early days of women's lib, asked for my father the alum's endorsement as I requested admission as the first woman to ever enter the geology program. My father's adherence to principles and values has influenced and remained in my heart for life. He combined a fun-loving character with strict work ethics, and he was always close to our activities. I have fond memories of him getting up early on Sunday mornings to help me as a young child with a school project and then making waffles for breakfast for the family. Away from my father at this point, all the conversations with him, who invariably had an anecdote about his own father illustrating beautifully a point about his deeply held values of honor and respect and integrity, would flood my memory. It just seemed so incongruous to me that those same values would be disregarded in an institution such as Stanford.

I struggled between my principles and the reality of life. I was aware of the values and principles that I held dear, and acting with integrity was one of them. In the end, the pull of my principles was the stronger call. It was clear in my heart: If it came to that, I would rather leave Stanford without a Ph.D. than accept conditions that I deemed unethical. I sought out two sounding boards: Andy Bateman on the outside, and a member of my research committee, a professor of petrology and field geology known for his independence and forthrightness, on the inside. After full disclosure and reflection, both of them shared my position, and with their encouragement I filed an official complaint with the dean of the school of earth sciences. The dean took the matter with the seriousness I felt it deserved and remained poker-faced. He invited me to appear at a meeting of the full school faculty, where I would present the case and await resolution. And so I did. I presented my case and waited outside the room. The joint faculty decision was expedient and Solomonic, disapproving of my advisor's behavior, requiring him to support me through the current life and subsequent extension of the NSF grant, and forbidding him from appearing as coauthor on any publication on the subject.

It had been a difficult struggle, and the tension it had generated would not dissipate for years. But it was reassuring to be supported by the school. My fellow students applauded with surprise and joy, the school had upheld its values, and I had a lighter feeling in my heart that allowed me to continue on with life.

Live Values That Liberate Creativity

YOUR VALUES DEFINE the culture of your organization and must be lived—reflected in every action—not simply framed and posted as examples or imposed as rules. Rather, they need to be defined and discussed first, accepted by all, modeled at all times by the leader, and insisted on without exception. This insistence is what positions values as the foundation of the culture of a group, and their reflection in every act or choice of every member of the group is what cements that culture. This is, of course, of paramount importance for you as a leader, as everything you do is an example: people in your group look at everything you do and take cues from every one of your gestures. Therefore, to be effective in creating a culture, you must live and breathe your values. This is hard to achieve if the values of your organization are not your own—those you can truly live without compromising, those you can celebrate and support through time. So define as values for your group issues and aspects of life that you, as a leader, hold dear, beliefs and principles that you care deeply about and *live by*.

> Among the members of the glass group, there was cynicism and doubt when I first took over as their manager. Whether it was because one of their peers was now their supervisor, or because I advised them that I had a more hands-on approach than my predecessor, they questioned: "Can you be our leader? Can you inspire us?" As is common practice for many leaders, my first meeting with a new group included a presentation of values and expectations, and it was then that they started to form an answer, as the discussion on values helped set the stage for the mutual understanding and trust that is the basic element of working together. Through give and take they not only came to understand and accept the values I was setting in front of them, as well as my expectations, but to understand that my hands-on style was not meant to be hovering over their shoulders, but rather guidance, coaching, and judgment on priorities. The rest of their answer was the day-by-day maintaining of their trust that was my responsibility.

Our values, the principles we deeply believe in, the issues that are important for us to stand for, do not necessarily remain constant throughout life. Some may evolve, others may be added, others still may be dropped. There are those, though, that do remain unchanged. Those are the ones that as leader will be more meaningful to you and therefore more powerful in creating culture, the ones you need to establish in guiding your organization. In working with many groups of scientists and in seeking to nurture creativity, I have found those values essential to me, and I have shared them as groups rally around them. At the core of the sphere of values are those that rely on qualities of the individual:

- Transparency
- Integrity
- Trust
- Passion

These four core values need to be embraced by each practitioner and lived through each one of their actions, and they must underlie the values that guide the way individuals behave toward each other:

- Respect
- Interdependence
- Freedom

Similarly, the core values need to underlie those values that practitioners bring to activities and assignments:

- Flexibility
- Rigor
- Fun and play

When all the above values are moving synergistically, results are delivered, emerging as a value themselves: that for which the group strives.

RESPECT

Respect for ideas, for needs, for the whole self, is where it all starts. For the human being, the productive artist, the jazz singer, the heart surgeon, the architect, or the creative scientist, respect is what creates the space that allows conception and invention to flow. Respect is expressed by the leader in multiple ways. It is in the everyday exchange, in the interest in stopping by their offices and inquiring about their lives, in understanding their worries, concerns, and needs. But, most significantly, respect is expressed by understanding their call for space and independence.

"I Don't Need You"
Honor the Creatives' Need for Autonomy

The glass research group was regarded in Corning's technology community as the hardest to manage, equal parts brightness and roughness. As I started leading them, I would tell myself, "These scientists speak their minds. In seeking to understand nature, their job is to be skeptical and to challenge the system. How can we pay them to do that and then expect them not to behave similarly within the social system of which they are a part?" It was easy to tell—they would volunteer it at the right moment—that they did not have much use for people like me, not me in particular, but the role of the manager. And often, they were right.

Legendary senior scientist Paul Genetti, watched and followed in the lab by senior and junior researchers and managers alike, would express this need for space more directly and vehemently than most as he said, "I don't really report to anybody. I don't care who my boss is. I can't be managed. I can just be suppressed and frustrated [by managers]."

Respect for this crucial side of their nature—the need to feel untethered, the need to safeguard their autonomy—takes the form not only of understanding that this is not a personal rebellion against you as a leader, or a deficiency in adjusting to a group setting on their part, but rather that it expresses a need to achieve that sense of empowerment that constitutes an important driving force for creatives.

So the challenge posed by a group that sees little use for managers, the challenge to the leader, is to not take it on *as a challenge*, but to take it for what it is: an expression of that need for uniqueness of the creative spirit, a protection of the space essential to invention, or the face of independence. Or a blending of them all; these are traits seen in the brightest of spirits. That the yearning for autonomy is being expressed in your group is a measure of your ability to not squelch debate or box them in. If you are at this stage, congratulations. You are laying the foundation for a culture where innovation can thrive.

Having viewed the need for autonomy for what it is, it is easier to move away from the battleground of control. Feeling at ease when not hovering over their shoulders, responding to their views and needs on timing and resources, or leading them to follow their intuition are expressions of your ability to move from engagement to detachment, from the arena of control to that of empowerment. Scientists, like any other human beings, perform best when they are driven by inspiration. It is the same in an artist, an architect, or a surgeon. We depend on their creativity. So tell the people in your group, "If you think something is really important, follow your heart. It energizes you, and you give your best performance." That is the way of allowing creatives to be "on a roll," what for athletes is commonly regarded as "being in the zone."

From the challenge of respect for autonomy it is all downhill to expressing respect for new ideas that come from "left field," whether it is a request for fewer meetings, or for less frequent reporting on activities, or for a different venue for the summer picnic, or a new concept or approach to an urgent situation. Expressing respect is not just about creating the space for ideas or opinions to be vented. It is about being *open to accepting* different views and putting together the elements to *make them happen*. And being open to accepting does not mean being agreeable all the time. It means just that, being open to engage in a dialogue, to evaluate pros and cons, to win some and lose some. By engaging in dialogue with openness to counterargumentation, you, as leader, will be modeling the behavior that is the ultimate goal of the value of respect: respect for each other.

FREEDOM

As the acknowledgment of autonomy, freedom is the other side of the coin of respect. It is the maximum reward; it empowers, it respects, it recognizes. Freedom starts with forms as basic as freedom of style. Few things express so clearly who we are and what we stand for as the clothes we wear, daring or conservative, carefree or careful, lighthearted or serious. And feeling welcome to express something as basic as "who we are" is a *sine qua non* of finding our creative juices. So do not just give lip service to this personal expression of being; allow the hallways to become a runway where styles are celebrated. The knowledge you will gain from this understanding will be invaluable to your ability to lead creatives.

Project Runway
Rejoice in Attire as an Expression of Self

We had scientists whose style remained a constant. Whether coaching a soccer match, melting glass in his lab, making a presentation to upper management, or attending visiting hours at a funeral home, you could expect to find Brian MacHarg in his favorite outfit: corduroy pants, rolled sleeves on buttoned-down shirts, Adidas Samba indoor soccer shoes. It was his way of saying, "I am true to myself and have little regard for convention, expect nothing but my honest truth." And so we did, because we knew who he was, as did he.

Then we had those who surprised us at every turn. Take Maggie Russell, a technician in the characterization sciences group, who had a collection of shoes rivaling that of Imelda Marcos. There were pink and yellow and green flats; black and white and multicolored shoes; blunt-toed and pointy heels. Most she bought, but some she painted herself. And she was careful to match them in color, style, and message to her outfits. It was just sheer joy to watch her walking down the halls or taking the elevator. The message was clear: "I am light-hearted and vibrant, willing to make the extra effort and try new things." And she did, and she was able to influence results and teams, to lead initiatives in the lab and out in the schools and community.

When Kirsten Steinmeier felt comfortable enough to come out of the closet, she started wearing the outfits she had longed for: simple, belted dark slacks with impeccably ironed white shirts, manly wool blazers, and heavy-soled laced black shoes. With her new style, her demeanor changed. She exuded confidence, standing tall, shoulders broader than before. She was telling us, a smile dancing on her face, that "I have made it." Somehow, for a reason still unclear to me, she never did wear the ties she fancied. To encourage her I would at times wear a button-down shirt with a skinny men's tie in a matching color, make a point of visiting her office, and, in an attempt to entice her, invite her to wear matching tie outfits one day. It never worked then, but I am confident that she will wear one when she is ready.

And leading the parade, I relished the opportunity to design and materialize my own weavings and garments in colors and textures that were limited only by my imagination.

Another expression of individuality, one that creates the unique atmosphere that can be inspiring or demoralizing and thus must be given unbounded freedom, is the personal office. Though office space and design can vary widely in personality, from the fancier corporate labs that must often follow canons of design to the haphazard arrangement of boxes in garages that typify entrepreneurial settings, what should not vary is the ability of each resident to make it uniquely hers. Reflecting the respect for the individual in the group's selection of design for the workplace impacts directly the culture of the group.

Making It Home
Celebrate the Uniqueness of Their Workspace

In the labs in the United States and in France, Corning has individual, hard-walled offices with internal and external glass windows to maximize inspiration as well as concentration while enabling a sense of connection to the rest of the group. When the U.S. research building was being remodeled in the late 1990s, in an attempt to keep up pristine appearances, the operational group created a policy that forbade researchers from putting anything on the walls. Envisioning bare walls as appealing and inspiring as those of prison cells, and anticipating the strong reaction of all to this straitjacket, I pushed back to change the policy. After much argumentation, the facilities group could see the point and yielded. Today scientists have made their offices uniquely their own. Some are decorated with carefully placed artwork, others are totally plastered with maps from all over the world; there are those that are lit by lamps with warmer incandescent light bulbs; and, in one case, a tropical rain forest of potted plants welcomes you as you walk in.

Then, occupying a category all on its own—unique enough to have been featured in an article in *Fast Company*—there is Peter Murray's desk. I used to call it the geological cross-section from the Archaean to the Recent. The foot-high stacks of paper are held in place by glass samples and may be punctuated by a radio playing classical music, his lunch for the day, or whatever else occupies his mind at a given point. It is his unique archiving method, and it works for him; he seems to be able to find whatever he needs on the spot. "I can always tell when someone has disturbed the force," he will tell you. Clean, and you will disorient him. And that is fine for this creative mind.

What the highly educated, highly skilled, skeptical personality who finds no use for managers is really wailing for is freedom from restraints. Beyond restraints that suppress one's style or expression or use of space, the most suffocating of restraints is that on time. I do not mean to advocate technology delivery in the absence of timelines. More than the elimination of deadlines, what the creative mind needs is freedom to allocate its time. Ideas and the passion behind them need the time to flow, and the experienced creative mind knows well how to manage time between well-defined short-term deadlines and unbounded greenfield research. The notion that researchers should be "free" to do exploratory research on Friday afternoons is ludicrous and needs to be replaced with the notion that researchers should be free to do exploratory research *when the inspiration strikes.* Freedom. Inherent in it lies a paradox: innovation *requires and provides* freedom. Once the space for innovation has been found, freedom provides a "cocoon" for creativity, engaging the total being. A prized cocoon where time goes by unnoticed, the energy stays high, the concentration disconnects you from the world. Those who have experienced it—what Mihály Csíkszentmihályi describes as a state of "flow"—know it. And, as leader, it is your most precious responsibility to help those in your team find it and, once found, to protect it.

Not all your team members will have the same need for freedom, and only your deep knowledge of them as human beings and of their track record will inform you on the size of the performing ring each needs. For the truly creative with the best track records, the ultimate freedom goes beyond time and becomes a need to choose research. In the glass research group, the first assignment to those new hires in whom we had detected a passion to explore and the ability to be at ease in pursuing "unguided" research would involve at least half of their time as unassigned time. The experience is not a test where there are right and wrong answers. The most creative find an untrodden path that ultimately leads to a new technology, a new solution, even a whole new class of materials or area of research. If guided, protected, and, yes, pruned, they may grow to be significant contributors. But finding that this is not the case, that a given researcher prefers the more structured environment of an applied project, is of significant value to them and to you. Knowing them allows you to place them in the right assignment, the right role, the right setting.

To Each His Own
Create and Defend the Space for Talent to Unfold

Within months of arriving at Corning, Rabbindrana Raja, with his sophisticated understanding of glass structure and properties, and with my comment that "finding a glass that could deliver ultra-low transmission losses is the holy grail of optical fiber" as his only guide, came to my office to let me know that he thought he had a way. Although he could not guarantee it, guided by basic scientific principles and a bit of data, he "just knew" that his understanding could guide us to develop a new product, and Corning would go on to prove soon after that he was right. Just like him, at that point we had no guarantees either, but we just knew that this was the start of a productive career, and he went on to become a prolific scientist, as his trail of publications has proven.

By contrast, Ben Pulanski, equipped with an equally sophisticated understanding of glass structure and properties and trained by the same advisor at Stanford University, when given the same initial freedom, quickly understood that he relished the world of applied research; for him, hitting the target properties is exciting, the challenge of manufacturing requirements stimulating. And he was right, as his career of contributions to applied glass projects has demonstrated.

The ultimate reward for those scientists at Corning who make it to research fellow—the highest rung of the technical ladder—is the freedom to pursue research of their choosing. These are researchers seasoned not only in exploratory research, but in delivering tangible technologies. As they are given the space to follow their hearts, they attract younger scientists who are motivated and inspired by them. In emulating them, in learning from them, and being coached by them, the circle is completed.

The ultimate freedom, of course, is the freedom to stay. The first time my groups heard me say, "You owe it to yourselves to explore other opportunities and to be here because you choose to be here, as your arena is the world," they would often receive it with surprise. But I really meant it, not as a way of pushing or challenging them, and neither with braggadocio, but with the feeling that comes from somebody who has given the best effort to grow and develop every single person to her highest potential, and to create the best possible culture, jointly with them. And from somebody who knows that unless every single person in the group is there because he *chooses* to be there, that goal will be harder to reach.

FLEXIBILITY

Respect and freedom open the way for flexibility. Flexibility to embrace new ideas, to accommodate life needs, to change direction, to change your true-and-tried ways. Flexibility is the way of life in research, so leading your group to adopt it as a way of life *in life* will bring vitality and a "can do" and "why not?" attitude to your group. It is an important culture-creating value as it shifts the focus from the "what" to the "how." And, just as importantly, it touches lives in all dimensions, from trivial to crucial.

IMPACTING CAREERS

As the ultimate expression of flexibility, I believe it is our job as leaders to adapt our management style to the individual personalities of those in our groups—scientists, technicians, administrative personnel—rather than the other way around. This is not about being wishy-washy or inconsistent in your ways. It is also not about making it easy on you. It is about having the flexibility to be exactly the best supervisor for a given person at a given moment, which translates into every single person having a supervisor with a different style. Not a supervisor with different values, views, priorities, or expectations, but rather a supervisor *who is also* an individual coach.

Personalized Leadership
Know Them and Inspire Each in a Unique Way

When I was given responsibility for the Inorganic Technologies Directorate, I brought together three research groups reporting to me: glass research, ceramics research, and process innovation. To lead these groups I selected three very different individuals, with very different experiences and different personalities. I soon found myself using a different approach to lead each one along the path of becoming a leader who could take a creative group to its highest level. At staff meetings they would all be exposed to the same strategic direction, expectations, definition of roles and responsibilities. But, in one-on-one meetings, my manner of approaching each was chosen by their needs and reactions.

Jacques Montebourg, the superb clarinet player who came from the research center in France with some experience in functional management, already had that "why not?" attitude, was willing to try new things, and had enough self-confidence that he didn't need to prove himself. Because of his engaging personality, his interest in people, and his ability to motivate them, I tasked him with turning ceramics research—a group that was singly and successfully focused on the support of one of the business units, the environmental products division—into a group with broader focus in the large and fertile area of ceramics. The goal was a group that would feel the freedom to explore different compositions and different processes, a group that would untether itself from the tie to one composition and, by exploring the vastness of the world of crystals, open new worlds for Corning. Jacques needed little direction from me other than continuous reinforcement of his self-confidence and some early pointers in getting to know the people in his group, some of whom I knew because I had previously been in that group. In a short period he had demonstrated an ability to put his arms around the technology and to create links in the organization, to align himself with the organization and play his role, and to understand and manage group dynamics, create identity and motivation, and embrace creative conflict. He did all this with an unencumbered personal style that made things happen. So I gave him rope, watched him from a distance, and saw his group react positively to him. We were on track and there was little for me to do beyond being supportive and removing barriers.

To this day Jiabao Lu has not let me forget that I was taking a risk on him when I first made him the manager of process innovation, as he had never managed a group. But I had seen him— a bright, hard-driven, fearless scientist with a Ph.D. from a major university in mainland China and with a forceful way of expressing scientific views that were most often correct but less often popular—perform as a technical contributor and inspire teams to deliver hard-to-reach milestones. I had remarked on his uncanny ability for abstract thinking and problem solving, his ability to take a myriad of complex problems, rationalize and prioritize them to structure sequential activities, and arrive at a solution. I could sense that "there was something there." His was a group that I had recently created with a goal that was new to the technology community: a research team devoted to early-stage process research. Jiabao's role was to transform it from an amalgamation of separate engineers and researchers who had little experience working together into a group that could invent new revolutionary processes for all of Corning's different businesses. Eager for the new opportunity, he was ready for the task. And he soon proved it, putting together teams, defining goals, proposing approaches, and creating projects. His group responded enthusiastically.

His peers and upper management, however, were having a more difficult time understanding his hard drive and oftentimes forceful delivery. For in his zest to make things happen, in his zeal to leave no stone unturned, Jiabao was not aware that his actions were "less than subtle." He was regarded as aggressive and hard to deal with. Up close, I could see somebody eager to make it work. I could also see somebody who could take it. I could be—and would be—brutally honest with him, giving him clear, unsweetened feedback and direction. I could even hit him with the proverbial two-by-four and he would not turn defensive, but instead would welcome the sense of awareness he was developing. He would be willing to go back and make amends, if needed, or to change his course of action. We had long, frank conversations—punctuated with explorations of culture or language tutorials—that as a result of his receptiveness were productive.

His group was delivering and motivated, and he was being challenged and growing. It worked. For this is the style he needed: up-front and honest, with reassurance but also with demands and expectations. And in the same way that managing conflict feels uncomfortable and is a behavior that is often avoided even though it is essential in leadership, being candid and straightforward may not feel comfortable to many a leader. But it is another essential skill to develop.

Manuel Cáceres, the accomplished Andean musician we had recently hired and given responsibility for the glass research group, had what was regarded as the hardest group to manage: a group of talented scientists, not unlike those in the other two groups, who delivered technology to all the divisions in the corporation and who were used to speaking their minds. Pile on top of this the need to understand the "whats" and "hows" of his new multidimensional role—corporate alignment, driving results, group dynamics, principles—and you have a steep hill ahead, particularly if this is your first climb. So I was supportive but demanding of him. Over the next eighteen months, Manuel was coached by Dasa, our guru; by Ned Ashton from the office of the CTO, who knew the people and culture of the lab better than anybody else; and by the HR community. I played an intensive, often painful, game with Manuel, giving him rope and letting him hang himself, pulling him back in and coaching or admonishing him, sometimes gently, sometimes bluntly.

Early on, it was much easier for Manuel to worry about counting the number of people assigned to projects, as constantly demanded by an overwhelmed organization in hyper-growth, than to take the time and extra effort that delivering technology through developing people takes; he found it faster to go around his chain of command to get a quick fix than to align with it, easier to understand the technology than to advocate for it. The dimensions he was leaving behind are important ones in creating and leading technology, and I was relentless and exacting: I would not give them up. It was frustrating for all—for scientists and directors as much as for Manuel himself—to be aware of his unseen potential and not be able to support him to realize it. And, though the process of bringing the potential out was trying and contentious at times, we plowed through, feeling that the investment was worth it.

It took time for Manuel to let his innate ability rise to the surface and allow it to become second nature, to move beyond that compelling sense that he had "made it big" and could therefore "be his own man," as he was used to from his entrepreneurial days. In time, his ability to inspire people prevailed, his understanding of navigation within a large corporation increased, and he found his role within the organizational structure securely. Today, under his leadership the glass research group continues to deliver steadily, without a hiccup, addressing the hardest challenges that the display and energy markets have come up with.

As for the culture of the group? The clearest answer came after ten years, at the holiday party that Manuel organized for his group. Dave Johnson, the fundamental scientist–gourmet cook, made a point of taking me over to the side to tell me: "Thanks for bringing Manuel to lead the group. I never thought it would be possible, but the culture continues to be what you yourself would have created." Shortly thereafter, Manuel closed his remarks and acknowledgments to his group for another terrific year by addressing them briefly: "And, finally, to all of you, for yourselves, for your trust and your performance, for the technology we have delivered together, I thank you for making this what has been the best job in my life."

PERKING LIVES UP

Another aspect of flexibility impacts the daily lives of creatives. Flexibility to accommodate life needs is an established concept in the American workplace. At Corning, the practice of allowing personal time to ease the stress of medical visits and sick children enjoys wide acceptance. What makes flexibility a value in addressing time or other issues is the willingness to stick to it through thick and thin, to support the scientist who has moved his mother home for her last six months with a terminal illness, or the recent widower who for months can find neither solace nor inspiration. And what makes flexibility a value worth having is the willingness to create the space for receptivity and the chutzpah to address the most unique of situations while staying true to your other values.

Easy Fixes
Have the Agility That Delivers Solutions

A couple of years after hiring Isabel Lopez, the talented fluorine chemist from California, I noticed that her vitality appeared to diminish during the latter part of every winter. It was not that her performance was suffering, but I could detect a lower level of energy and enthusiasm. I went in to talk to her and she opened up to me. Yes, she had been dragging, feeling uninspired and dull. No, there were no medical reasons, as a battery of tests had proven. Located in upstate New York and with a dense cloud cover, Corning "enjoys" many long months of winter, during which the sun hesitates to appear. We wondered together if these first exposures to shorter days and diminished sunlight were causing seasonal affective disorder. There was only one—easy—way of conclusively proving it: to give her additional time off to spend a week in the sun of the West Coast in the middle of March. The effect on her was immediate. When she came back, the jaded young woman was gone, and our lively Isabel was back. An easy solution, one earned by her, and with a windfall profit for the group. In future years, rather than giving her a cash award when she deserved one, it was clear to me that for Isabel true reward came as a certificate for an extra week or two of vacation, rather than as a check or stock options.

In addressing an issue of a different nature, finding a solution to the dilemma of lack of health insurance for Kirsten Steinmeier's partner was also easily found. While Corning's leadership debated the pros and cons of extending to the entire company domestic partner benefits to the gay community, I—acting within the purview of a group manager—made sure that awards to Kirsten, earned through her performance, were generous enough to leave sufficient funds after payment of spousal health insurance coverage.

AS YOU LEAD, SO WILL YOU HARVEST

"Love pays back love," or so says the Mexican country love song. Similarly, after experiencing the effects of a leadership style that is tailored to their individual needs and allows them to develop and grow, to feel respected and to enjoy freedom, scientists will gladly turn and respond in kind and exhibit the same flexibility. Even if it means having to venture outside their comfort zone as they pitch in and carry the load, the sprinter will participate in the marathon, the diver in the relays. If the culture you have established is strong enough, it will stretch and yield while maintaining its strength.

There Is Payback

Practitioners Live by Your Values

Corning experienced a near-death experience as a result of the collapse of the photonics bubble at the turn of the twenty-first century. The ensuing painful process of workforce reduction forced us to choose not between the good and the bad, but between the good and the excellent. In the aftermath, my supervisor and I pondered how to align our resources so they could help pull the corporation back to the arena of growth.

Even though we were responsible for research and hence the future of the corporation, it seemed clear that we had to allocate resources to address the immediate needs of manufacturing, which after all was part of our mission. We also knew that only a focus on manufacturing excellence—with the improved near-term productivity and resulting profits it would deliver— could yield the immediate pull to take the corporation out of the deep hole before its expiration date. This was in contrast to the culture of long-term research that we strongly believed in, that we had ardently established and fought for, and that the corporation also believed in, as evidenced by its long-term tradition of supporting research with "patient money." The answer, then, called for a temporary retreat from an emphasis on fundamental research to a focus on not just applied research, but manufacturing excellence research. With our reduced numbers, the big questions then became "how many?" and "who?" Driven by his desire to provide freedom and maintain vitality, my boss, while understanding the urgency of the situation and choosing between two risks, fell on the side of offering a reduced number of our fundamental scientists to the effort. Sitting on the other side, and emboldened by the deep understanding of each one of the scientists and the culture we had created together, I countered, "Why don't we put them *all* in?" And so we moved.

Without a second thought, the scientists and technicians all responded with enthusiasm. Understanding the gravity of the situation and their ability to make a difference, not one hesitated. Focus was changed for all. People moved from developing thermodynamic models that explain defect formation in fiber to recommending the atmosphere for consolidation conditions in fiber draw manufacturing; from developing novel, hot-stage microscopic techniques for studying batch-melting reactions to optimizing sand dissolution during glass melting for bubble elimination in making precision glass at the plant; from modeling photonic crystal fibers to improving boule quality for high-purity fused silica through the purification of bait sand. Anybody previously exploring new materials for amplifiers, or pursuing a fundamental understanding of fluorescence gain or lifetime, or crystal structure issues pertinent to the photonics world transitioned to developing new glass compositions for the display sector. Researchers exploring coextrusion of different materials, or fundamental colloidal precursor ceramic formation, moved to the batching, drying, and firing of honeycomb ceramic substrates in manufacturing.

In one of his visits to the lab at the time—a time of severity and shortage, reflected even in our presentation that day when we had to leave behind the customary large, printed fancy posters and instead use single PowerPoint pages glued onto posterboard—our CEO was pleasantly surprised with the new emphasis for research that the inorganic technologies group had found. The search for fundamental understanding had given way to the prominence of the much-needed research into manufacturing excellence at the moment. What was a true revelation, though, was that rather than the anticipated atmosphere of duress and sacrifice stemming from scientists whose work at the moment did not reflect the true nature of their passion, what he encountered was interest, curiosity, and enthusiasm. And deeper than that ran the sense of satisfaction that comes from knowing that you are crucial in pulling the boat into safe haven, which is exactly what they were doing and what they kept on doing for a period of time, after which, to the relief of all, the emphasis was turned back to fundamental issues.

FUN AND PLAY

There is an air of lightness that the creative mind craves. Walk into a roomful of inspired artists and you will sense it. It is an energy that allows the creative spirit to free itself from limitations, that enables it to envision the changing of context and conditions that is a prerequisite to invention. Fun and play, in bringing that nimbleness, that buoyancy, help to maintain the spirit that invites novelty to emerge.

Carrying on social activities, even corporate-dictated ones, as a group and bringing to them the lightness and creativity to turn them into truly fun events allows the group to experiment with combinations of social forms and rules that would not be conceivable in the everyday world of organization. But, as discussed in the context of culture creation, in addition to bringing lightness and nimbleness these fun activities have a powerful impact on culture definition as traditions of celebration that help create that culture.

Ornaments, Trinkets, and Cakes
Let a Rich Imagination Be Your Guide

One of the favorite get-togethers for the glass research group was Secret Santa or, as I liked to call it, "Getting to Know You." I had first enjoyed this holiday tradition at the Max Planck Institüt in Germany, and I brought it into the group with one specific instruction: once you pulled a name from the hat, you had to learn about the recipient—likes, interests, hobbies—before choosing a gift. We would set an afternoon aside, bring in home-baked goodies, play music, and let the fun start. Everybody had to guess first, from the clues provided by the giver, who the recipient was. No one was exempt from jokes. And the fun did what fun always does. Flying in the face of social hierarchies while sitting on the floor around the room, we were able to put together connections between elements from the lives of fellow workers that we had not seen before: Hemingway and the sarcastic scientist, merengue music and the mechanic wizard technician, china teacups and the office manager. We made jokes, took the time to explore, and simply had fun.

Holiday parties—fancy in times of largesse, pot lucks in times of duress, but always with the entire group, spouses and partners as well, all dressed up as much as they wanted, with good food, music, and dancing—moved from being compulsory and boring to becoming lively and fun. At Christmas time, there was always a nonreligious ornament for everybody, in glass of course, often designed and made by our own scientists and technicians, at times using one of the new glass products that had been launched from our group.

Goal-sharing check distribution events saw decorations with paper money floating all over the place and cups full of chocolate coins, and make-your-own-sundae stations and cookies and goodies. All this continued to create that spirit of joy, to allow us to get to know each other better, and to create ties that brought trust.

And then there were the birthday celebrations, where roles were reversed and the free improvisation stretched the ability to deal with change. As with other celebrations, in good times we took an order from the "birthday child" for their favorite scrumptious cakes from local bakers, and in harder times we would take turns as bakers. Seeing the men stay behind when it came time to cut and pass out slices of cake, I banned the women in the group from performing these tasks in an attempt to reverse double standards. It was fun at first to see the guys performing these small chores, cutting slices that Emily Post would have to make efforts to accept, keeping track of who wanted what. In the end, they were all better for having mastered a new skill.

Each group has a different personality, as does each leader, and so there is no limit to the activities that bring fun and play. Once I was asked by Jiabao Lu, the forceful scientist from mainland China, to attend a breakfast meeting with his process innovation group. Expecting the usual bagels and cream cheese, I was pleasantly surprised as I walked into the room to find Jiabao himself turning pancakes for all at a large griddle he had brought from home. They were tasty and we all enjoyed them, but the lasting value was in the playfulness, the change of roles and context that Jiabao, the leader, was bringing to the group, and its impact in liberating the creative mind.

So go ahead and be playful. Bring activities that liberate creativity. Put yourself as leader in the position of coaxing your group to experiment with unconceivable social rules, to envision bringing together dissimilar elements in looking for solutions, and, in so doing, to enlarge their view and promote their intensity of response and flexibility. No, you will not be "exposing yourself." You will be opening yourself, showing your fun, charming, unencumbered social side. And, in prolonging the spirit of play, you will reap the results, for when the most challenging tasks are carried out from a work spirit of joy, they are play.

INTERDEPENDENCE

Put a roomful of bright, driven, and creative characters together, throw in a good measure of freedom, turn on the music, and what you will have is a group of independent prima donnas dancing around each other. Or so is the vision—the nightmare actually— that often pushes hard-driving managers to resort to boxing-in behaviors. Creative minds are fertile and often supple and responsive. And so the concept of *interdependence*, though initially counter to their notion of *independence*—which they deeply cherish and protect at all costs—and closer to that of *dependence*— which they abhor—can and will be followed as we guide them to honor and develop it.

The principle of interdependence can be philosophically as complex as one's foundation permits around the concept of seeing every member as an inseparable expression of the whole, with distinctions of form within the totality but no real separation into parts. Or it can be as simple as the recognition by individual members that in the workplace their survival, success, and well-being depend on the mutual reliance of a collaborative group. Honoring interdependence does not negate the ability to act with autonomy—that is, to be independent—but instead brings in the additional dimension of awareness of the impact of your actions on the well-being of the group.

Let's Fly Together
Mutual Reliance Brings Muscle and Choice

When Paul Genetti, the charismatic and independent-minded physicist, traded his usual rebellious demeanor for one of mending bridges during his confrontation with the patent department, he did so after arriving at the awareness that the members of a truly effective team are interdependent, with their personal success and survival, as those of the group, depending on their mutual reliance and respect. His ability to put his bright intellect into venturing into a previously unexplored concept trumped his need for independence.

In my process of leading Corning's European center for technology through significant change and after sessions on strategy, behaviors, and expectations, my staff came to realize the significance of shedding their attachment to the independence they had long cherished and embracing instead a spirit of interconnectivity and reliance on each other. The understanding of how their actions affected each other, and their ability to drive new behaviors of mutual reliance and collaboration, not only brought the lab to a whole new level of impact and productivity, but it gave my direct reports that very elusive feeling of freedom and independence that they had been afraid of losing.

In practice, honoring interdependence starts with self-managing, self-motivated individuals coming together to constitute a successful team of supportive, responsible individuals committed to one another and to their purpose. The goal is not about generating a "do good, feel good" atmosphere. It is about success and survival. Highly competitive individualism can hinder or destroy teamwork and undermine the trust essential to organizational flow and morale. The interdependent group, by contrast, has conquered the challenge of discovering the balance between individuality and collective purpose, between self-interest and the aim of the group. Work thus flows unencumbered, as individuals empower the whole group to attain greater internal effectiveness and respond more appropriately to challenges.

Whether in the simplicity of execution or in the complexity of intellectual discourse, interdependence is a powerful concept, one that I encourage you as a leader to add to your list of values. Resisting interdependence only creates ineffectiveness and dysfunction in the system.

TRANSPARENCY

I favor the value of transparency over those of communication or open communication because it conveys the intention as well as the deed of exchanging information openly, of not holding back, of honesty, sincerity, and candor, of no hidden agendas. It is a value that is the essential underpinning of a good number of others; it is hard to feel respected where there is a lack of transparency. Absence of transparency betrays integrity, and ultimately, trust is built on transparency.

As a leader you owe it to your people to be transparent about your intentions, your plans, and your concerns, in the same way you owe them your expression of your active interest in them, their results and careers, in the form of direct feedback, dialogue, and give-and-take. And though these give-and-take sessions can at times lead to difficult discussions, they are the first steps in creating a culture of open, honest communication. Do not be afraid of the quirky, moody humanity of your people, but rather embrace it and learn to revel in it.

"How Does It Feel?"
Cultivate and Express an Interest in Their Lives and Views

In leading my groups I believe in being in close touch with people as human beings. I feel it is important to know about the family situation of every one of the people who worked in my groups. To know what kind of work environment suits them. To be able to see when someone is not motivated. One of my tools is the simple question, "How does it feel?" I enjoyed walking into someone's office and asking, "How does it feel? How does it feel in this project? How does it feel in life?" I would have this conversation often with people, not just people whose performance concerned me, but all of them. It invariably opened up to rich— and sometimes hard—dialogue. I also knew that it was important not just to ask the question, but to listen to, and handle, the answers.

A dimension of transparency that is often hard for leaders to practice is exposure of their vulnerability. The sharing of concerns, of unmaterialized plans, and even dreams can be regarded as a risk to the image of strength pictured for the leader, or as compromising her ability to create a vision and be followed. But, counterintuitively, the courage that it takes to open up and expose what concerns you as a leader—and what concerns you as a human being in your personal life—will turn apathy into appreciation and motivation. And your team members will emulate that same willingness to be entirely open to fear and go right through it, truly establishing you as their leader.

And How Do *You* Feel?

Be Comfortable Sharing Your Own Life and Views

I had been responsible for Corning's center for technology in France for more than a year, leading it through significant change with enthusiasm and determination. From the strategic direction to the definition of competencies and the support of the business units, I was energized by all dimensions and was moving along, addressing them jointly with the leadership team I had defined. It was not easy, as change seldom is. At one point I was feeling disheartened by my inability to change the culture of my leadership team. I felt that my efforts in moving them from the hierarchical space where the authority figure provides opportunities and resources—where they were comfortable—to a space of empowerment and accountability were yielding little fruit. It felt to me that all the effort and resources I was putting behind this cultural change were in vain. One morning, at one of our staff meetings, I opened up to them and shared my feelings of disappointment at not being able to noticeably move the needle. I was not surprised by what ensued, a rich discussion, albeit an unexpected one for some of my staff members, you could say even uncomfortable for others. What I was not prepared for was the surprise the next morning. On reaching my office I was greeted by a beautiful handmade ceramic vase with a flower arrangement as only French florists can produce. As a lover of art, I was touched by the thoughtfulness and beauty of the offering. What moved me, though, was the accompanying message, from one of my staff members who had mostly stayed quiet during the discussion of the previous day. It simply read, "Thank you, Lina, for opening yourself to us and teaching us about leadership." It warmed my heart.

So turn your concerns and fear into energy, and open up to sharing your dreams, your difficulties in realizing your plans, your unease in turning the tide. Once you have opened up, the "How does it feel?" question can and will be turned around to face you. And you will find views and opinions that differ from yours and that, coming from a different perspective, will help you stretch. Do not bind yourself into thinking that your perspective is the only valid one, but instead open up and allow these transparent exchanges to keep you on your toes. Take advantage of the individual and collective wisdom of your group and their unique perspectives, and heed their advice.

It is without doubt much easier to be open and communicative in times of success and plenty, but it is ever more important to be so in difficult times, when economic strains dictate harsh measures that may even affect your group and you need to maintain the confidentiality of sensitive information. This is the time that calls for greater transparency. I do not mean to suggest that transparency is about divulging all the information that crosses your desk or about sugarcoating the message in an attempt at protection. It is about having the respect for your people to understand that they have a right and a need to know, the wisdom to discern what will guide them from what will distract them, and the dexterity to convey the message in a productive way.

INTEGRITY

Corning is a corporation that has clearly spelled-out values that steer both large-scale external actions and everyday internal activities. Values are displayed throughout its offices and plants, are discussed by top leadership and middle management alike, and are lived. My creation of values for our groups was not meant as an act of independence but, rather, as a way of bringing concordance between specific values and mission to a group. In this way, values become the foundation for the culture of the group. I made it very clear that within our groups, living the Corning values was taken for granted. No need for duplication.

I made, though, one exception to this unnecessary doubling up, and it was to include integrity—the bottom line of Corning's values—among our group values. It was not just the bottom line for our groups as well, but it was intrinsic to the way we needed to operate: in truthfulness and sincerity. To live the value of integrity—the willingness to give and keep your word, to walk your talk, to fulfill your promises and agreements—is in essence to live in your commitment. And, as a leader, this is your aim for yourself and your people. Integrity is an unforgiving value, one that may exact unyielding pain if not pursued relentlessly, as the

smallest of exceptions may give rise to damaging effects and consequences.

Technology-driven companies live and die by the strength
of their patent portfolio. Their ethos places great values in patents;
careers are made by them and businesses are created and destroyed
by their defense. So in a company like Corning, which invests a
healthy dose of sales into technology development, making sure
that the patent portfolio is aligned with business strategy and that
patents are rock-hard defensible is a must. Claims must be clearly
spelled out and documented, *and* inventorship must be unquestionable. From the social aspects of innovation this matter could be
a hot potato were it not so clearly spelled out by law: an inventor
is that person who contributes at least one *original* idea resulting in
a claim, rather than the person who makes it happen. But struggles
happen and can be so taxing as to tempt supervisors to gloss over
them and just include the entire working team as inventors.

Whose Invention?
Have the Courage to Address Thorny Issues

We had a productive scientist at the lab, Ronald Quinby, a valuable inventor with the ability to understand a situation and apply
the right technology to solve a problem. An electrical engineer
with a gregarious personality, a musician, avid hiker, and fit
sportsman, he enjoyed connecting to everybody as much as he
enjoyed the freedom granted by his many solutions to manufacturing problems. Ronald was one of a small number of people
who had the freedom to roam around the building, sniff out an
interesting problem frustrating any given team, and go at it in
pursuit of his solution. And he would almost always come up

with something. These results would more often than not require patent protection. On one occasion, the team receiving Ronald's unsolicited help had some members from the ceramics research group, which reported to me. As the patent was being drafted, I heard the cries of dismay from my researchers who felt strongly that Quinby had contributed only by implementing their ideas, not by generating any original ideas of his own. It was a long and arduous battle, figuring out exactly the very important who-contributed-what-and-when that can invalidate a patent if not captured correctly. It involved not only interviewing scientists and technicians, managers and patent attorneys, research, development, and manufacturing, but ensuring that different versions of accounts and dates matched. And it was not a popular battle—it would not earn anybody any brownie points—but it was a battle worth fighting, as much for the validity of a patent as for the preservation of the value of integrity. And on a deeper level it was for the trust of the researchers in my groups who could continue to be confident that they had somebody who would go to bat for them. In the end, the validity of the patent could not be questioned on the grounds of inventorship: only those contributors of original ideas were included—thus, not Quinby.

Flexing your muscle to keep the playing field safe by refereeing conflicting inventorship claims, and recognizing the rightful inventors publicly, is worth all the pain it may bring to the life of a leader. Giving creative, gregarious personalities space to spot out problems and enough rope to investigate is a clever way of finding solutions to tough issues. But if there is no guidance to the personality, the risk of this approach is to allow someone to believe that he is larger than life. It may feel more comfortable for leadership to give untethered rope to big contributors than to rein them in, allowing them to become "untouchable." But it backfires for the rest of the organization; faced with a situation where contributions are minimized or hijacked, the creative spirit shrinks. Having the leader step in and set the record straight restores the sense of being and brings the confidence and trust back.

PASSION

Our role as leaders is to serve and support people to succeed. And nothing helps a human being succeed better than finding the core energy, the force that underlies all actions, the main driver that is his passion. Ideally, as beautifully said by Robert Frost, the goal is to unite avocation and vocation because it is then, when we love doing what is required, when work becomes fun, that the endeavor of life is truly accomplished.

As a leader you are in an enviable position to help people unite their avocation and their vocation, and by so doing make work become play. It starts by using your intuition to become aware of the unseen potential in others and to support them to see and realize it. This is not about influencing their consciousness with what would be your personal choices, but about opening them up to their own.

Understanding your calling, choosing the fork at a junction, or starting a career journey can be fragile moments along a personal path, with unique expressions for each. There are those who arrive at the door with a clear understanding of who they are, where their energy stems from, and where they are headed in life; there are those whose lives need to explore many stages, learning and contributing at each and always growing; and then there are those who take their time in agony and search, who need guidance and support at every step. There is a tenderness and vulnerability when people are expressing a new aspect of self or a new way of being that we need to protect until they grow strong enough to take flight on their own. As leaders, our role in each case is to actively mentor and guide them into the personal path of their own discovery and, inasmuch as they are driven, their own awareness.

Follow Your Heart
Advise and Guide Without Imposing Your View

Throughout the years, I have served numerous people as mentor and coach. The situations have been all different, the personalities even more diverse. The request for advice, however, often comes in the same form: "What should I do? What would *you* do? Would you explore development or stay in research? Push against the manager or join him? Take on this new job or endure the travails of the current one?" And my answer would be consistent: "What I would do is not important. What matters is how you *feel* about it. What would you *love* to do *now*?" For therein lies the truth to our search. Find what you would love to do *right now*, let that intuitive feeling guide your decision, and, one step at a time, tread the path of your passion and your life.

As a leader your reach extends to identifying new career opportunities that can be explored and to providing the support and the resources that people need to perform successfully at a high level. This may even mean that you help someone find a passion that leads her outside of your group. Yes, part of the creation of a culture that does not stifle creativity is the making or finding of opportunities that will result in your losing your superstar so that she can spread her wings and fly high. This is an exercise in authenticity, one that is counter to the misguided coaxing of a scientist with leadership abilities, whose true calling is science, into helping you with your supervisory load and enticing him with the vision of making him a manager.

TRUST

Trust is that fragile and vital value that must underlie every activity but that cannot be tangibly created. Trust is also essential to high performance. But there is something elusive in grasping it. We understand its many definitions. We know it just develops. We appreciate that it cannot be taught. And we accept that it must be earned. Earned by repeated fulfillment of expectations, by supporting intelligent risk taking, by recognition of another's contributions. So instilling trust in your group is done gradually, with persistence and consistent behavior. Ultimately, the values of transparency, integrity, and respect that you have defined and lived provide the foundation for trust.

Expressions of trust are recognized by everyone's willingness for open, honest communication, dialogue, and feedback. They can be found in agreements that are kept by all, they are at the core of the courage of taking intelligent risk, and they underlie a sentiment of mutual respect. These are the behaviors of a group that has reached the point of mutual trust. When you spot them in your group, you will know that the work has just begun because, just as you do of them, they *expect you* to trust *them*. And this needs to be reinforced daily.

The utmost expression of trust is the willingness to place our future in somebody else's hands, to follow his guidance into unknown territory, to pursue a trail that we had not chartered or even envisioned ourselves.

Dancing with You
Creatives Learn to Trust and Follow

The willingness of Tim Cobb, the physicist and ballroom dancer, to shift the focus of his career from fundamental mathematical calculations to applied projects upon my advice, was an expression of trust that opened his life to dimensions unforeseen by him, dimensions he might not have experienced—interaction with others and valuable guidance to others—had he not developed the trust and taken the risk.

The Ultimate Act of Trust
Practitioners Have Your Back

I got to know John Taylor when the melting engineering group joined the glass research group and became my responsibility. With interests ranging from antique car rebuilding to sailing, playing the cello, and singing, the gathering of his attributes defied definition and was certainly at odds with conventional engineers. For John brought together the rigor of the engineer, the creativity of the artist, the high energy of a teenager, the passion for ideas and concepts of the inspired, the willingness to address people and issues of the connector, the belief in the future of the dreamer, the confidence in people of the altruist. The altruist and the connector in him would at times combine with unfortunate consequences, for his intentions were often ahead of his tact.

He had the awareness to see this, explaining, "If I mess up

something, I don't necessarily have the ability to fix what I mess up." So we developed a close relationship as I guided his path. There was no need for me to lead his technical course, for he was a strong technology leader in the area of glass melting who could quickly find direction and chart a route to delivery that was as revolutionary as it was technically sound. His transition from melting research to chemical burner approaches to glass forming was seamless, and he rapidly started to expand, stirring up collaborations and initiating contributions with other projects and groups. What I would more often do was help him navigate the intricacies of roles, participation in teams, human intentions, and diplomatic approaches, so that his novel ideas and proposals to others would yield the intended results. And it was a delight to see him mentoring people, leading discussion groups, creating a working environment of motivation and enthusiasm.

His influence and connections went beyond Corning to span the globe, and he established himself as an effective agent of change in glass-melting technology delivery throughout the world. He relished the environment and was brimming with passion and enthusiasm for what he was doing. And he was motivated by the insistence on excellence and trust. He had learned to trust his colleagues, his environment, his leader. But his unconditional level of his trust would surprise us all.

John Taylor understood the level of pain that a leader experiences when facing major cutbacks in personnel. He saw me forced to choose, keeping the wife while letting the husband go, retaining the father as the son was let go. In a gesture that not only displayed his generosity of spirit but also his belief in the group, he approached me with an offer to take early retirement so that other, younger creatives could be spared. "The decision," he said, "is up to you. I trust that you will do what is in the best interest for all." In his trust, John was giving me the ultimate freedom to make a life-altering decision for him as a symbol of his utter support. I would not do it; I would not make this decision for him. It was his alone to make. Though much time has gone by, his level of trust moves me to this day.

Not that he was ready for retirement. His level of activity following his decision is proof of where his interests were, and still are. He continues to be active in glass-melting technology, leading international committees, consulting with major glass companies throughout the world, stirring thoughts and projects in pursuit of his vision of changing the way the world melts glass. And I continue to enjoy his passion and his dreams as he shares them with me.

RIGOR

Meaningful scientific investigation is pursued by adhering to the scientific method—observation, hypothesis, experimentation, results, and theory. Deviation from this method can result in bypassing important elements that may invalidate an outcome. Following it rigorously is therefore a must. And so it is with any team trying to achieve results than can be reproduced time after time, which is an imperative of innovation, whether on the manufacturing floor, the construction site, or the operating room.

As the fundamental quality of good scientific work—and good work in any field—rigor is not only a necessity but an ultimate element of culture. By insisting on it rigor permeates the thinking of a group and comes to represent an important underlying principle of every activity. As discussed in the context of demanding excellence, rigor thus comes to mean not settling for just OK, or "good enough." Rigor translates into being clear in communicating the difference between dreams, hypotheses, theories, and results. Rigor insists on dotting the i's and crossing the t's of a new process. Rigor results in documenting results and recommendations thoroughly. Rigor produces fully developed scientific theories, discussion of results, and publications. The net result is credibility, a culture that can be trusted, results that can be relied on. This is the basis of support for your group from the larger organization—and from customers, clients, patrons, or benefactors—and thus is the basis for your group's long-term endurance. Insisting relentlessly that rigor underpin every word, deed, or action by each and every group member is worth every ounce of effort, for the staying power of your group rests on it.

RESULTS

For any team chartered with delivering innovation, whether in high technology, medicine, or cinematography, the raison d'être is bringing forth results. There is a delicate balance—the "creative tension"—between unleashing creative researchers and harnessing their work to deliver actual products and revenues. Stifle creativity and you get predictable, marginal progress that does not create competitive leaps; let freedom run rampant, and you risk developing something that customers can use or will pay for.

Two elements are important in cultivating a culture of results. First, there needs to be breadth in the definition of "results," and this does not mean a diluting effect but a definition based on the true understanding of your mission and the means of achieving it, and then there is a need for identification of the whole spectrum of desirable results. Tangible results, those that customers will pay for and use and the processes to make them— such as the optical fiber they rely on to bring information to their home, the new cardiac surgery technique that can save lives, or the new building design—are easy to classify as results.

But these tangible results are not created in a vacuum. There is a body of understanding behind each product and process that is pulled along by jumps in fundamental understanding of underlying and surrounding sciences, arts, and techniques. And for the vibrancy of the group and the establishment of the larger organization as a leader in the world, any product of this under- standing—a patent application, a scientific publication, a presenta- tion to the international scientific community—also needs to be valued and publicized, for these are the links in the chain that pre- cede and lay the foundation for the final breakthrough.

And then, of course, the element of recognition and reward is what completes the circle and brings the impact of the result back home. It is true that the achievement of the result is in itself a compelling driving force for the creative mind, a powerful intrinsic motivator, as Amabile has articulated. But the experience adds another dimension through the recognition, celebration, and reward of the accomplishment. Recognition helps make the pain and duress, the challenges and argumentation that are the daily lives of innovation team members, ultimately worth it. So, make every effort to create a culture that understands impact and identifies results, that recognizes them both in private and in pub- lic, and that rewards them accordingly. There are opportunities both large and small to create this environment in all organizations, opportunities that languish in smothering cultures but that become occasions for celebration in fertile, motivating cultures.

Be relentless in adhering to the values you have established and in standing up for them, even when it is inconvenient, even when management is pulling you in other directions. You are leading brilliant people who catch on quickly if your values are something you are willing to compromise. Standing firm on these values is the cornerstone of building a creative culture in which your teams can thrive. It will take all dimensions of your personality: energy and humor, courage and objectivity, thoughtfulness, and even charm. Your people know it, and you will gain their respect by holding firm. Yes, things may be painful for you at times but you will be leading by example, they will follow, and when needed will be willing to do things that may even bring pain to them.

Demand for Excellence in the Tropical Rain Forest

IN CONVERSING WITH GRADUATE STUDENTS I like to remind them that despite the drudgery of graduate student life, in their future they will cherish those days and remember them as some of the happiest ones of their lives, when they had freedom of choices and few constraints. I had the influence of two persons, my external advisor Andy Bateman and his wife Cathryn, an accomplished weaver with a zest for experimentation with every textile-manipulation technique possible. She opened the door to the world of weaving and gave me the wings to explore what became a lifelong passion for creating original wearable art that has at times kept me afloat when I would otherwise feel like sinking. Because of these two complementary influences, my recollection of graduate school is one of liberation, of opening new doors and new worlds with new perspectives and new activities. And it was with this spirit that I carried on as I embarked on my new adventure as a postdoctoral fellow after finishing at Stanford.

Years earlier, while still a college student in Colombia, I had read an article published in the early 1950s by a geologist who, while doing exploration for Shell Oil, had found some unusual rocks on the island of Gorgona, then an uninhabited island some forty miles off the Pacific coast of Colombia. With nothing of the like having been reported in the scientific literature at the time, the rocks remained for years unclassified, more a curiosity than anything else. They were intriguing, and I stored them in a mental filing cabinet, where they were still within easy reach as I started reading papers and hearing lectures at Stanford about komatiites, certain rocks found in Archaean terrains—earth's most ancient—and exhibiting mineral phases and textures that brought to my mind those from Gorgona. Could one group those unclassified rocks with the komatiites that were being first described from South Africa and Australia? The presence of komatiites—which represent lava flows requiring very high temperatures for their formation deep within the earth—was considered restricted to the oldest terrains on earth, terrains that had formed when the internal temperature of the planet was still high enough to generate these unusual lavas. Thus komatiites were thought to be incompatible with young terrains. But from any and all geologic perspectives it was impossible to regard the formation of the young island of Gorgona as having taken place any time geologically close to the Archaean. As enticing as it felt, the paradox was one that I was in no position to address then. Writing a Ph.D. dissertation had higher priority.

I could not wait long enough to unpack my boxes when arriving in Washington as a fresh postdoctoral fellow at the Carnegie Institution before presenting my proposal to Pete Brauhoff, a German geochemist with whom I was to work. With a broad culture, a sharp intellect, and as much gusto for life and good wine as he had for pushing the edge of geochemistry understanding, Pete attracted an entourage of the best researchers as collaborators, and being around him was as upbeat as it was demanding. He eventually rose to become the head of one of the Max Planck institutes in Mainz—easily the best-endowed national research organization in the world at the time—and to receive international acclaim. So his enthusiastic response to the idea of exploring the Gorgona rocks was a powerful motivator, one that would drive me to follow him to Germany after three years.

By the time I arrived in D.C., the government of Colombia had established the island of Gorgona as a place to house its most dangerous prisoners. The island had been named after the gorgons—the monstrous women of Greek mythology with snakes for hair—by a crew member of the Spanish conquistador Pizarro after the expedition lost more than 60 percent of its crew to deadly snakebites when they stopped to rest on the beckoning tropical island. Clearly, the Colombian government was not mistaken in its judgment that deadly snakes, tropical rain forest, and waves beating against high cliffs would create ideal conditions for the country's tightest-security prison, one on par with Devil's Island.

Logistics for travel, stay, and fieldwork on the island demanded both persistence and ingenuity, and these were my responsibility as principal investigator. For my first trip—I was to return for later trips with a six-month-old baby in tow—I managed to recruit Carlos Vélez, a seasoned geologist from the Colombian geological survey with proven connections and field experience that served us well. I had gone along with Carlos's suggestion to invite Eduardo Limón, a researcher at one of the universities in the country with a long-term interest in the biodiversity of the island. The island was served by primitive boats leaving twice weekly—or less frequently as we were to find out—from the port of Buenaventura, propelled by loud engines, indiscriminately carrying passengers and freight, and taking sixteen hours to make the forty-mile crossing. And in this manner we started as a party of three.

Upon arrival, we found all our needs met. The army major responsible for the penal colony assigned us to the priest's house, one of sixteen carefully aligned structures that made up the town, and enlisted one of the trustees—a prisoner nearing the end of his twenty-seven-year sentence for murder who had significant prior guerrilla experience and would make a good guide in the surrounding jungle—to serve as our field guide. To ensure our safety he called on one of the young prison guards to join us, armed, on our daily expeditions. The last detail, the one life-saving detail that concerned us, proved tricky. Access to a working refrigerator for night storage of the snake antivenom we carried with us on our treks was not the issue. The problem was ensuring the low temperature required by the antivenom in light of the need to shut down the island's power generator after midnight. Hoping for the best, we took our chances.

Exploration of the island turned out to be a unique experience, a mélange of rock outcrops, monkey tracks, machete-opened trails, coconut water, thorny palm trees, slippery slopes, high cliffs, menacing waves. It was an experience that filled me with excitement at every discovery of the rocks I was after, and some that nobody would have predicted. There was much ground to cover and I did not want to miss a single outcrop. This was not the time to slack, and I demanded the best from the team.

During lunch breaks in the jungle we would learn about the life of the rain forest from our guide, who educated us on the many poisonous species of snakes we encountered, whose names we had never heard, and whose markings only he could distinguish. While trekking, we would walk single-file through the opening left by his machete and, following his advice, take turns being second behind him. His reasoning—that the sound of the machete awakens the poisonous snake from its sleep and the following footsteps alert the animal to take a striking position from which its jaw can reach the third set of passing legs—made sense to all of us. A few days into our fieldwork I could hear behind me the rhythmic sound of clapping. Not occasionally, but continuously throughout the day. Eduardo, as it turned out, was developing a phobia of snakes and his clapping was aimed at scaring them away ahead of the machete. We would try to distract him during the day, let him take the third position behind our guide all the time—away from the position of potential bites—reason with him at night that it was a low-probability event, to no avail. Rather than getting used to the situation with time, he began to lose control. His irrational fear started to have an impact on the team, and soon Carlos and the guard were wondering if we should just stay away from the interior and its jungles and restrict ourselves to exploring the perimeter of the island, the sandy beaches with their tempting coconut groves. It was clear that Eduardo's fears were having an effect on the mission.

Geology is a science that builds on interpretations made from observations, data, and samples collected in the field. The quality of fieldwork is dependent not just on mechanical observations and the collection of rock samples. It requires scientific acuity of mind to be able to work and concentrate under challenging physical conditions. A mind cluttered with fears, logistical details, or other distractions is prevented from the abstract thinking that allows an interpretive image to emerge from the analysis of details of the few data points found in the field. Eduardo's behavior was not just eroding team morale; it was directly affecting our ability to concentrate and intuitively access information, and compromising the goal of the expedition itself. His minute-by-minute distractive behavior made careful observation of the nature of the unique rocks that made up the island difficult and understanding their relationship close to impossible.

Consultation with Carlos gave me his perspective: Though he was a senior geologist, experienced and tough, he did not think it was in our best interest to hurt Eduardo's feelings. For me the situation was clear and I had a different perspective. Although I was by far the youngest member of the professional party, responsibility for the success of the expedition fell squarely on my shoulders. Gorgona was not an island that one could visit on a weekend getaway, and, given the potential significance of the work, the success of the mission rested on maintaining the team's ability to deliver excellent results. From the army major in charge of the penal colony I found the schedule of incoming boats. And so Eduardo found himself boarding the next boat to dock in Gorgona and heading for the mainland of Colombia.

Postscript—Our years of work and publications on the geology of the island went on to show that the intriguing rocks from Gorgona were indeed komatiites, a discovery that demanded different theories for their formation.

Luckily for all, we never had to use the snake antivenom we continued to carry around.

Demand Excellence
and Enrich Lives

ASSEMBLING THE BEST and the brightest and defining values provide a strong starting point for establishing the "persona" of a group. Coaxing your group as individuals and as teams to let their intuition and drive guide them, and creating the space and freedom for their talent, rigor, and creativity to bear fruit, are further important elements. An additional and important ingredient, one that is significant in balancing the need for green space with the superiority of results, is to create a way of life of high expectations and full engagement. The challenge for leaders—as Peter Block would say—is to pursue our vision with as much courage and intensity as we can generate.

Demanding excellence is not about creating a cult of perfectionism, but instilling a spirit of high performance. It is as much about anticipation as about results; it lies at the intersection of the "what" that is being done and the "how" it is being achieved. In leading groups, I learned from Dasa that high performance is about focusing on commitment and contribution to make it happen rather than on the need to prove self-worth; about pride in self-worth taking over doubt and low self-esteem; about bringing enthusiasm and a positive attitude to counter anxiety and fear of mistakes; about personal learning from mistakes rather than blaming, punishing, or invalidating the other; about seeking continuous improvement rather than letting the "get it done and over with" tendency limit you. And, having reached the goal, high performance is about celebrating success rather than experiencing relief by the culmination of the effort.

As with living your values and with everything you do, in inspiring a spirit of high performance and demanding excellence, as a leader you need to guide, direct, coax, detour, show the way. And to do so, you need to lead by example. So set expectations that are your own, that you believe in and look ahead to living and guarding with the same zest you had when you ushered them in. There are two critical elements for success in bringing out the spirit of high performance in your group. First, expectations must be clearly spelled out, not just on your first day as a leader, but for every single assignment, project, and suggestion. Directly and to the point—and directly to the receiver. And be sure to ask if it is all clear, as it is often easy for the creative mind of a leader, in the excitement of a new idea, to get carried away in laying out all of the "whats" and to pass over the "hows" that are expected. Failure to be specific about expectations only leads to confusion and frustration on all sides.

The second element is, naturally, consistency—though not rigidity—in upholding your expectations. Clearly your knowledge and understanding of each one of your team members—their interests, their skills, their desires—should inform your selection and opportunity assignment and hence your expectations. Your expectations may be nuanced by the people, the circumstances, and the activities they perform, but your expectations, like your values, should not be accommodating of personalities, true for some but not for others. Few things can be as destructive to team morale and performance as the existence of "untouchables" who can do no wrong.

At the core, the leader needs to offer unconditional support and a deep interest in the careers of practitioners in such a genuine way that it underlies and permeates each action and is deeply felt by everybody. All other behaviors of the leader must follow this spirit and must all support the team, with the overall effect being the living of a culture of excellence where all behaviors raise the bar for each other.

It is essential for the commitment to excellence to run in two directions, thus creating a culture of accountability where the sense of empowerment entitles practitioners to expect excellence from the leader as much as the leader does from them. For this to take place, we as leaders have a responsibility to our teams to clearly identify our expectations and to offer behaviors that will support the team, with the assurance that they, the practitioners, are entitled to expect these behaviors from us.

In making it clear to practitioners that I expected them to use their skills and follow their instincts, go the extra mile, and achieve mastery, I would commit to support these behaviors by knowing each one of them, understanding and managing their dynamics as they work together, and designing teams that work, as well as by recognizing their achievements and contributions and "advertising" them throughout the organization.

Similarly, in making it clear that I expected them to be flexible and adapt, benefit from argument, and have some backbone, I would pledge—again—my commitment to know individuals, teams, and dynamics to be able to support them in their efforts at stretching and pushing themselves, and to do so while recognizing and celebrating their idiosyncrasies. These are daily exercises in guiding, persuading, and showing the way that, offered as your commitment as leader to them, allow them to trust your sense of accountability.

EXPECTATIONS OF A LEADER

There is great richness and importance in keeping the bar high and in letting high expectations, for rigor and for results, permeate all team activities. Define and pursue those principles of excellence you believe in and that you can uphold with vigor. If specific principles and behaviors are not clearly defined, the concept of excellence will stay as a backdrop rather than permeating every day and every activity. At my first communications meeting with my groups, they consistently heard me articulate that I expected of each one of them:

TO USE THEIR SKILLS AND FOLLOW THEIR INSTINCTS

There is an inescapable connection between honoring your being and doing good work. It is only by playing in the field where your skills are found that work can become play and you find yourself giving your best performance. I place great worth on this and provide much support—personally and through other professionals and advisors—for individuals to release their potential for professional effectiveness and personal growth. But this is a personal search that cannot be enforced. I expect every member of my groups to have the interest and the gumption to be aware of what their skills are and to hone them, and in so doing to allow themselves to be guided by that unexplainable internal voice that says, "I just know it, though I don't know why," and use their expertise to get them there. I expect them to know where they excel, to use their expertise to get there, and to follow their drive to reach beyond. This will take them where nobody else has been before.

TO BE FLEXIBLE AND ADAPT

The ultimate expression of rigidity is rigor mortis. Along its path one only finds lost opportunities and lost friends. So in the social process that is innovation there is little value in being set in your ways, unable to look at things in a new way, unwilling to listen to an alternate viewpoint or to take a new path, or unwilling to take an unusual assignment. And I mean this both in the social and in the technical context. I expect people to be willing to push themselves out of their cradles of comfort into the heat of the midday sand, and jump and dance if necessary. To reach out and connect with groups they have never heard of, to go out of their way in welcoming the newcomer. To vibrate with different music and try a new ethnic food. And to bring all of that newly acquired richness back into the lab as a new scientific perspective, or just as a new tune to hum.

TO GO THE EXTRA MILE

With the perspective that the number of failures in *any* attempt at delivering a breakthrough venture—whether in architecture, medicine, or science—far outweigh the number of successes, in innovation "good enough" is only that. It does not take you to the goal, it just leaves you where you are. So push yourself with enthusiasm, with determination. Make that extra effort hard enough to make it happen. And do not leave your wings behind. Take a risk while you are at it. No, I do not expect anybody to jump off a cliff to prove bravery. But I do expect them to live the value of rigor already discussed to its fullest by not settling for "just OK" and to push themselves and their performance up a notch. I also expect them to have the courage to take responsible risk, just not the lack of sense to commit professional suicide.

TO ACHIEVE MASTERY

My groups have heard me exhort them many times: "Become an expert and let the world know about it." Assembling the best and the brightest in the world is the first step. Putting together all the elements for them to free up their potential is a good second step. But it will only go so far if they do not do the rest: become the best they can ever be. I have expected every single person in all of my groups to play his part in becoming an expert at what he does, and in letting the world know about it. The definition of "world," of course, varies with the individual. For some it may the lab, for others the corporation, and for yet others the international academic and scientific communities. But the expectation of being active in a community and striving to lead it, of establishing oneself as *the* expert on a given technique or measurement, the person to go to for new equipment concepts, the administrator that can solve all the issues, or the scientist leading the international community, does not change.

As with other things, my focus on mastery is not just about reaching for the goal—the "what"—but about the motivation behind it—the "why." It is not about indulging or, worse yet, encouraging a need to prove self-worth, nor is it for the flattery of recognition. It is understood by practitioners that mastery is an essential ingredient of creativity, as it provides the means by which ideas materialize. But it is important to take it beyond expertise. From the perspective of expectations, mastery is the opportunity you get for the creative space that is being provided, the opportunity to take it beyond just knowledge, expertise, or superior skill at a task. My expectation is that mastery become the integration of insight and experience, wisdom and skill. I expect from the members of my groups the merging of professional excellence with personal fulfillment, and thus I expect to see their actions flowing spontaneously and appropriately; this is what mastery looks like for the professional, the cab driver, the copy editor, or the athlete.

TO BENEFIT FROM ARGUMENT

Ask any young scientist preparing for her first presentation at a national meeting what her main concern is and she will say that it is not about knowing the material—she should know she is the world's expert in her own area—or the quality of her presentation, but the questions that she might be asked: "Will they be harsh or lively? In disagreement or support? Who will come after me?" are the thoughts racing through her head and making her stomach uneasy. Though just jumping into the ring, a young scientist knows already that argument is the essence of scientific discourse. The challenge of dissent, the impact of rebuff, needle the researcher as much as her own curiosity does in the pursuit of answers. Because of the importance of maintaining a vibrant, challenging environment, a give-and-take that keeps us honest, I expect people not to shy away from conflict *and* its resolution. This is a particularly important point in organizations such as Corning that have "polite" cultures, which strive to avoid arguments. I do not advocate argumentation for the sake of fun or as a way of exerting control. What I expect is to have the clarity of thought, the courage of spirit, and the ability to articulate a different viewpoint, to do so with an engaging dialogue, and to express it with a constructive tone of voice. Yes, there are those whose ability for debate placed them on their college teams and whose voice can carry a stadium. I expect from them to tone it down into a constructive dialogue. And I expect the rest to stand up and not shy away in discomfort.

TO HAVE BACKBONE, A COROLLARY TO GOOD ARGUMENTATION

Be willing to stand firm for what you believe, to defend the merits of what you propose. Making things happen is not about recoiling; it is about pushing things through with courage and intensity. And no, this does not mean grudgingly or offensively, but assertively. What I expect is the strength of character that can express its determination in effective and persuasive ways.

TO RAISE THE BAR FOR THEMSELVES

To give your best performance on somebody else's watch is child's play. To deliver it on your own is a sign of mastery. So demand the best of yourself. On your own. All the time. And do the same for those around you, for this is what completes the circle in the delivery of today's goal as much as in your own continuous growth and improvement.

For strong, high-talent people with a lot to contribute, these high expectations are neither oppressive nor exploitive. Instead they communicate the depth and seriousness of your respect, for we only demand the best of those whom we regard as the best.

COMMITMENTS FROM A LEADER

On the next level, expectations are a two-way street. In the same manner that you, as leader, expect from your group, you in turn entitle them to expect from you. It is not for team members alone to make things happen, to make superior things happen; they must be able to count on you as leader. Our role as leaders is to go to bat for them, to play PR agent for them, to protect them, to get them resources. In the spirit of trust and mutual respect, it is only natural that team members be entitled to have the same high expectations of their leader, to see in leaders the spirit of high performance, with the same courage and passion as is expected of them.

As leaders, it is our responsibility to be accountable to each member of our groups and to let them know what they can expect of us. This starts by putting in front of them some of our responsibilities to uphold the excellence of the team and to expand the reach and range of their professional lives. In my case, in addition to carrying on the responsibilities of managing the group, I shared that they should expect of me:

TO CONTINUOUSLY RAISE THE BAR AS HIGH FOR MYSELF AS FOR THEM

I pledge to know each of them, what they can bring and what their very best effort is, and to drive them to achieve it. To guide them toward achieving mastery and self-awareness, without forcing them. And to demand the same of myself. When the going gets tough, it is at times easier for the cowboy to loosen the rope than to steer the bull. But for the committed leader there is no relenting.

Maintaining a commitment to excellence can at times bring pain to the leader. The constant act of pruning your group—vital to its development and growth—may at times exact the pain of needing to cut and let go of some of its members. But it is required of the leader, and not having the courage it takes and the wisdom to know whether to prune or to cut may risk team performance.

Even If It's Painful
The Agony of Leadership

In an attempt to find the spark and help him to reach his potential, I was asked to accept the transfer of Chris Benosky into one of my groups after what had been a frustrating year for his hiring supervisor. A bright young man, Chris had the drive to do something really unique that could have a big impact, the interest to get involved with experienced researchers, and the need for recognition, traits commonly found in driven young researchers. He had a reasonable scientific background and a gregarious personality, but what had been frustrating for his supervisor was his inability to stay focused on a subject and to engage in scientific discussions and articulate solid arguments. In those cases, he would retreat. Upon transfer to our group he developed a good working relationship with the well-known Paul Genetti, who was willing to mentor him scientifically. We were giving him our best shot, providing him the independence afforded to other new members in the group but staying close enough for guidance. Particularly, I felt that it was important to give him enough breathing room to contrast with the closer management style to which he had been exposed but had not responded to.

One of the most important attributes needed in our research groups is the ability to carry out independent research, and this turned out to be Chris's Achilles heel. His fundamental understanding lacked the depth necessary for adequate interpretation of data or for the formulation of truly original ideas. He lacked the rigor to go beyond postulating hypotheses based on observation—part of the scientific principle—to pursue further knowledge by data collection, modeling, study, or discussion. And he continued to be reluctant to take direction or follow the scientific lead of senior experts. The emerging picture was clear: the scientific understanding and skills were just not up to par. But if this was his Achilles heel, it was Chris's attitude that clearly marked the path. His receptivity to feedback, which could have greatly helped him improve his direction and focus, was compromised by his defensive behavior. My repeated efforts to move him to a space of awareness from where he could address beliefs and attitudes were continuously met with deflection and resistance. I had been earnest and fair, but in the spirit of commitment to excellence, I decided we could not afford to maintain scientists like him in a group focused on delivering the breakthroughs that were required of ours, and I recommended that we let him go. It was my first experience in dismissing somebody, and it was a painful one for me; for days

I felt a tightness in my heart every time I thought about it. The group was also shaken by a surprising reduction in size that was not driven by difficult economic conditions. In time they came to understand that the decision obeyed a higher imperative: the insistence on excellence.

Passing the Baton
Insistence Pays Off

Months after we hired Manuel Cáceres, the material scientist who succeeded me as manager of glass research, he and I were going through coaching sessions in a heavily invested induction period. Because the position was critical, we found ourselves considering other alternatives: removal and transfer. By that time, after often-intense discussions, we all understood in our hearts that we knew him and that he had unseen potential. I understood clearly that he had it within himself and that the pain and agony of demanding nothing but the best performance from him was well worth it. And so we pushed along, working on the nuances of alignment and interdependence, driving results and group dynamics, unleashing creative talent and complex requirements. It was intense, painful work, but time has shown that it indeed was all worth it.

Revving Up the Engine
Persist When the Prize Is Right

After some years, it was Manuel who was in the position of guardian of the tradition of raising the bar as he guided his scientific staff. He came to me in search of advice on his approach toward Dave Johnson, geologist and gourmet cook. Dave has an objective mind, an open spirit, and a happy-go-lucky personality, making him a pleasant package to deal with. In his research, he has a superb ability to apply his thorough understanding of basic scientific principles to the solution of practical problems. But it is a capacity he does not bring to bear on issues on a daily basis. He is just happy to go with the flow in a nonstrenuous way—though if you get him to engage, his delivery can be impressive.

We had seen this impressive performance from Dave years before, when representatives of Corning's U.S. optical fiber manufacturing plant made a presentation with a cry of help to the glass research scientists. For six months then—and six months of compromised production in the life of a plant manager is an eternity—the plant's only recourse to deliver single-mode fiber with enough strength to be accepted by their customers was to slow to a near halt the speed of the draw that pulls the fiber out of the last firing step onto spools for delivery. They were in a quandary. Speed up the draw to normal levels, and they would see the appearance of a silica-containing crystal phase contaminating the otherwise pristine ultra-pure silica glass. Slow down the draw and production and earnings dropped. Plant engineers—savvy, experienced technical personnel who knew and used every trick of the trade to maintain a first-class manufacturing facility envied by admirers and competitors alike—had tried all imaginable different conditions over the previous six months, but to no avail. Knowing his strengths, I was not hesitant when I walked into Dave Johnson's office, not with a request—which is more my style—but with a firm order: "You *will* solve this. And in no time."

It took Dave less than one week to understand that there was a condition within the draw that was leading to oxidation of the silica in the glass and prompting the formation of the crystal phase. One week, not because it was trivial, but because "he just knew it" in a way that only he could, by putting together the right perspective and the fundamental knowledge required. One week during which we saw Dave highly focused, engaged in enthusiastic discussions with colleagues during his coffee break, immersed in calculations in his office, showing up for work on Saturday mornings. And, of course, delivering well-documented cause-and-effect arguments. Plant engineers responded with excitement and support, and Dave followed with a full analysis of their draw conditions, putting in conference calls, videoconferences, trips down to the plant, leading to his identification of the specific conditions responsible for the issue and his delineation of the changes that would solve the problem. After their six-month wild goose chase, the plant implemented Dave's recommendations less than one month after their presentation to our group. To this day, the unwelcome contaminant has yet to return.

So Manuel and I agreed that to hone Dave's performance, to keep him at his highest level, it is necessary to keep him engaged, giving him critical problems to solve or create that meet his intellectual level and with a sense of urgency that puts his otherwise mellow personality in high gear. The uniqueness of the performance, the richness of his delivery, warrants it, and we set out to do that. Of course, just as the fanciest Bugatti engine would not survive long if kept revved up all the time, between the high-intensity peaks it is important to let Dave go back to the valleys of his curiosity-driven research at his own pace, for there is where he finds his strength.

TO TAKE A DEEP INTEREST IN THEIR CAREERS

Their careers are but a part of it. The commitment needs to be to take a deep interest in their careers, in their development as human beings, *and* in the whole of their life experience—and to participate by moving them along. To connect with their personal passions and resonate with them.

It should really be second nature for leaders to sincerely care for those they lead, to be interested in their careers and enrich their lives, and to be enriched by them. As leaders we are in a unique position of having knowledge of opportunities that match desires, of needs that fulfill dreams. And we can pair this understanding with the ability our position provides of moving people along to new destinations and increasing responsibilities. It takes a dose of creativity, some effort, and the interest to play your part, selling here, convincing there. If you join the game you will soon be expanding roles and enriching lives—yours as much as theirs.

The mutual enrichment of lives is not restricted to the workspace. If you have assembled top-level practitioners, you will have a group of smart, driven people who are going to excel in their careers as well as in their hobbies. Enlarging your own experience by learning from them is truly exhilarating: enjoying top-quality, fresh, home-baked goodies from your chemist, or the sounds of guitar strings from your polymer scientist, or a description of the mountains of Anatolia from your geologist are but the beginning. It will be your turn to have your own life enriched.

TO CELEBRATE THEIR PERSONAL IDIOSYNCRASIES

Beyond patience and tolerance, a leader must be broadly accepting of wildly different styles, rejoice in them, and use them to the advantage of the team or project at hand. Deeper than the acceptance of peculiar but significant behaviors, such as the messy-but-I-know-where-everything-is desks and of different working schedules, is the understanding and acceptance of the driving force behind each person and what each different person needs as guidance. Whereas one person may benefit from being needled to keep his fire alive and his sense of urgency awakened and at high speed, another may need assistance in keeping his fire at midglow, or his tendency to stir others under control, or his propensity to put more things on his plate than he can handle.

Controlling His Appetite
Guide Personal Project Portfolios

Whereas Dave Johnson's low-key driving force benefited from periodic revving-up to maintain the high level of performance expected and that only he could deliver, just the opposite is true of Peter Murray, his fellow geologist, brimming with passion, spilling with zest, overflowing with ideas. In his case, keeping him tuned meant just the opposite: it meant paring down his project list. When I first hired him, I would meet with him periodically, more often than with most others in the group, and ask him what he was up to. He would enumerate a long list of projects—assigned by me, created by him, requested as help, invited to join—with equal excitement for all. For Peter anything scientific is a riddle calling him, but a long list of these riddles can also become a stressful stack to handle. So I would proceed to prioritize them for him, making sure that I balanced his scientific appetite with the corporation's needs. More than killing ideas, the exercise was one of balancing. He would walk out of my office greatly relieved. And I would wait a few weeks, when I knew that we would go again through the same process. With time, I saw him learn to do this balancing act on his own. And today, as a research fellow, he actively mentors younger scientists to whom he assigns some of those project ideas that would clutter his plate before. He has taken his understanding of the need for balance to an extreme as he says: "My best role is to generate ideas, not necessarily to do all the work. Where I am now, it is crucial for Corning's sake and my own sanity to delegate juicy tidbits to young people who are looking for new opportunities."

TO DESIGN TEAMS THAT WORK

Allow creatives their personal styles, strengths, and needs to inform how they can be brought together in effective teams. Knowing and understanding each one of the players well enough to predict and manage team dynamics is the key to assembling a team with strong dynamics and interaction. Team members need to be complementary, but complementary disciplines alone do not guarantee complementary working dynamics.

Few things are as important in assembling winning teams as understanding team dynamics and putting the right person in the right role. Having two prima ballerinas in the same ballet only creates confusion—unless the objective is to end up with competing approaches and there is a competent project leader in place to aptly manage conflict, collaborate with functional leaders to manage personalities, and keep the project on schedule. Creating teams requires a sophisticated culture of assigned roles, links, and responsibilities, not only in the team but also in the larger organization. What should be uncomplicated to the leader, by contrast, is the knowledge of each person, her skill, her strengths, what she can bring to the table, and how to connect that experience to where it is valuable. It is not about assigning a warm body to a project or issue. It is about connecting the right person to the right situation—and every case is different:

Marathon Director
Look for a Thoroughbred You Trust When the Stakes Are High

We had a difficult project, one that ended up requiring the exploration of as many as eight different material systems—with as many technical experts—to respond to a competitive threat. To run the project I asked Jeff Major, a scientist with experience in research and development who had run several product development projects for consumer products when I was there. Though he was not in my group, I knew he was eager for a new opportunity. More importantly, we were peers and had known each other from my first days at Corning, so I had learned to trust his technical judgment, his objectivity, his backbone, and his willingness to take the heat. These four qualities proved to be the key to his successful navigation of the project and selection from eight down to the one final candidate.

Controlling the Switchboard
Find the Key That Opens Channels of Communication

The assignment of scientist-farmer Rick Laredo to be responsible for facilitating communication between the research and development organizations during a project to deliver new glasses for display applications solved a significant team dynamics situation that was hindering progress. But all it took was the understanding of the different players and their dynamics of interaction.

The Right Person

Knowing the Creatives Makes Play of Assignments

To resolve a manufacturing upset reminiscent of the single-mode fiber issue that Dave Johnson unlocked, assigning the right person took no longer than a few minutes. I knew instantly—because of her background and training on one hand and her most recent experience on the other—on whose door to knock. This time the plant was Corning's only fiber plant in the UK, which, due to a puzzling manufacturing upset was unable to make any multimode fiber, a fiber with a high cost driven by elevated levels of the expensive element germanium, but also a desirable high-margin product. After months of struggling, the plant was experiencing a debacle caused by iron contamination.

I was certain that Kirsten Steinmeier, clad in her black slacks and impeccably ironed white shirts, who was working on defect formation on fibers and who was our resident electrochemistry expert, could solve the problem. Plus, she was familiar with the manufacturing steps, the entire operation, and all the details that matter to plant engineering. What was more rewarding for me was to see the pace that her passion drove: she stayed up all night that first night, sending out an e-mail before dawn with her suggestions of conditions they could change. Received by midday in the UK, the plant proceeded to eliminate the offending step, one that involved the introduction of oxygen, and was able to resume production. Another case of the right person in research providing an immediate solution to a long-term, debilitating problem in manufacturing.

It all goes back to the golden rule: know the practitioners. Take the time to discover who they are, their strengths, their passions, and knowing which one to assign to play a specific role or be the saving force in a moment of crisis becomes child's play. Enjoy knowing them and your own life will be enriched.

TO RECOGNIZE AND ADVERTISE

It is a fact that the number of failures in the search for breakthrough innovation far outweighs the number of successes. Motivation, recognition, and celebration are therefore important antidotes against the doldrums of the valleys—the long valleys that lie between the peaks of success. And, though not every result is deserving of big applause, recognition has many faces: a certificate for dinner with their spouse at the restaurant of their choice; or the attention of an executive for smaller, less visible goals. And, of course, bringing the big guns out for the big accomplishments. So do not hesitate to become the advertising agent for breakthroughs and accomplishments big and small that your group delivers. Bring them to the organization, create the awareness in upper leadership of their successes and achievement, become the PR agent for the advancement of creatives. How else are their accomplishments going to be disseminated, their mastery established? This, in turn, becomes an investment in the future of your own group and its ability to survive in hard times.

TO GIVE THEM UNCONDITIONAL SUPPORT

Providing support is not about always agreeing or about cuddling or pampering. Yes, it is about having the best interest of your practitioners at heart and going to bat for their rights and about providing support for their projects. But it is also about being truthful and putting the mirror to their face, keeping your eye on the ball and being demanding with their responsibilities—and having them do likewise. Partly it is about teaching them to trust that if they fall when going out on a limb they will be picked up, and expected to get back on. But, most importantly, it is about supporting them in the process of growing and reaching their potential.

Unconditional support is a significant commitment from leader to practitioners, who after all are putting their careers in the leader's hands. The daily practice of unconditional support is an expression of values—integrity, interdependency, trust, passion, rigor, results—and its exercise touches lives, creates culture, and supports growth and evolution.

Years after his retirement, John Taylor, the cello-playing antique car buff engineer, kept alive his reaction to this unconditional support, still feeling the emotions as he described it:

You were so important to me, and to the majority of the people who had the pleasure to work for and with you, that we could not imagine doing anything that would disappoint you. Rob McLaughlin, the director of HR, told me the most important thing everyone needs is someone who is a constant in their lives. That is, a person who will support and be on their side No Matter What happens. They will always see the good in the person and be there if needed. You did that for everyone that reported to you. I've tried to do that, follow your example and be that rock with everyone I have contact within the lab. But I would not expect favors from you. I would expect you to tear into me or anyone in your group who failed to do as they have the capacity to perform. But, I know it would be a private reprimand, and it would be for mine or the person's own good.

So do not hesitate to give the practitioners unconditional support, true, kind, and tough unconditional support. The kind that will put them into high gear, drive them to deliver their best, preserve their integrity, enrich their lives, help them grow and develop, and—yes—make them feel loved. The organization will thank you for it. And you will have the results to show for it.

MY PERSONAL JOURNEY

Culture in the South Pacific

WE FIRST BOARDED the ship in the middle of the night as it waited anchored ten miles outside the harbor of Manila. As would be the case in many other ports of call to come during the cruise, the ship had not been allowed to dock because of the flag it flew. Crossing the harbor, we approached the ship in the dark on small outboard engine boats and climbed up the rope ladder that was thrown down the side of the imposing dark edifice in front of us. After reviewing and confiscating our passports, the captain of the ship officially welcomed us to Soviet soil. It was the mid-1970s and the world was mired in the Cold War, which would make for an unforgettable experience for everybody on board.

The 1970s had seen the geological plate tectonics revolution jump from country to country, igniting along its path the passion of scientists, academicians, and students alike and prompting and inspiring a surge in research and publications as never seen before or since in the earth sciences. Petrologists and geochemists joined geophysicists and oceanographers in their questioning of the earth in search for answers and missing clues for emerging theories. Field excursions to look for rocks would be followed by parties installing geo-phones. Dredging parties preceded deep-sea drilling initiatives. International congresses and symposia were musts for scientists hoping to stay abreast of advances. And countries, ignoring the call of politics, collaborated to make large-scale, large-budget proposals a reality. The International Geological Cor-relation Program was one such ambitious plan. As part of this plan, the *Dmitri Mendeleev*—a World War II vintage German warship that had fallen into Soviet hands and lived to see its transformation into an oceanographic research ves-sel—would sail between the ports of Tokyo and Sydney while dredging and analyzing rocks from the bottom of the ocean. The voyage called for forty sci-entists, half of them from the Soviet Union and the rest to represent the world, with experience in ophiolites—rocks formed as part of the oceanic crust now found on continental terrains and the subject of the international symposium I had helped organize in Colombia prior to graduate school. The cruise included lectures by the participants on board and stops at many ports of call for field trips to study ophiolite localities on land. An exciting highlight was to be the dredging of rocks from the Mariana Trench, the deepest part of the world's oceans. The provost at Stanford was impressed with my invitation to represent Colombia and lecture on ophiolite occurrences there and gladly funded my travels, enabling me to join other American scientists boarding the ship that awaited anchored outside Manila harbor.

Little could have prepared us for the experience. A boat large enough for the avid joggers of the 1970s to stay fit by running laps, with multiple decks where you would easily—and often—get lost, but small enough to be shaken like a flimsy canoe by the tip of a typhoon, as we would later learn. Exciting rocks, both predicted and unexpected, and interesting talks delivered with Italian, Czech, French, Russian, Swiss, Yugoslavian, Japanese, Italian, Persian, and Colombian accents. Food so lacking in vegetables and fruits to require three weekly bottles of Bulgarian wine delivered to your cabin in an effort to prevent scurvy—or so they claimed! On the day we crossed the equator, a bacchanal in honor of Neptune featuring a canvas salt-water swim-ming pool the size of a pickup truck, and flowing wine and greased sailors chasing scientists and crew alike and throwing them into the pool. And, as a memento of a day never to be forgotten, a multicolored, personalized diploma was presented to each scientist, showing the date and longitude of this north-to-south crossing of the hemispheres.

But not everything turned out as planned. Many countries at that time were more concerned with repercussions of the Cold War than with the advancement of science, and most of them denied the Soviet ship entry into their ports. The *Dmitri Mendeleev* thus was turned back from the ports of Shikoku, Japan; Guam Island; Manila, Philippines; Kalimantan Island; and Kendari, Sulawesi Island, Indonesia. After Manila, only the U.S. territory of Yap—the island with gigantic doughnut-shaped carved disks for currency—opened their doors to us. We stopped at the U.S. territory of Guam but were confined to international waters and not allowed to enter the harbor: the transfer of participants to land was carried out by a tugboat chartered by the U.S. Geological Survey.

The consequences were not just a matter of science, but also a matter of nutrition. Not only were we as scientists disappointed at not being able to look at real rocks in the field, but we were almost as distressed by what was coming out of the kitchen onto the mess hall, as provisions were running low because of the inability of the ship to dock on land. Andy Bateman, my thesis advisor and the American cruise leader who had boarded ahead of me in Tokyo, sent me a telex on a premonition advising me to bring on board as many jars of peanut butter as my bags would hold. By this time in the cruise, peanut butter on Russian pickles smuggled from the pantry by entrepreneurial and brave Russian scientists and delivered to Andy Bateman's deck-level cabin had become the highlight of our fare. The peanut-butter-and-pickle afternoons became our source of physical and emotional sustenance as, other than that, the menu consisted almost exclusively of dry rye bread, black tea, and cabbage soup. We were all at the risk of malnourishment—cultural, physical, emotional, and scientific malnourishment. Fortunately for everybody's scientific thirst the *Dmitri Mendeleev* proved successful at retrieving large samples of rocks from the bottom of the Mariana Trench, nearly seven miles deep and deeper than Mount Everest is tall, a feat considered highly unlikely before the start of the cruise. This revived our scientific spirits.

Cruising down toward Papua New Guinea on a Sunday morning, we were all hoping that Rabaul harbor would finally open its port to us. The captain had announced the possibility and everybody without exception was wearing their Sunday best and lining all deck railings as we approached the island. With Russian-held German Leica cameras pointing and shooting, we could all see the beautiful soft conic shape of the volcano that makes up that part of the island grow larger and larger, and we could hardly contain our excitement. And then, all of a sudden, we could feel the ship swiftly beginning to turn in a wide and open circle and the island beginning to shift position and to disappear from sight, only to reappear later behind us. Bewilderment invaded us, followed by indignation. The international community rebelled, demanding an explanation. But not so the Russian scientists. An announcement in Russian came on the PA system that prompted them all to quietly turn around and go back to their cabins. The captain had explained, we were told, that perhaps because port authorities in the tropics took Sundays off, he was unable to communicate with them, and international agreements precluded him from approaching a port without prior authorization.

As the Russian scientists were starting to come back up on deck dressed again in grubby work clothes, the international community, in search of honesty, followed Andy Bateman, who in defiance of the captain's authority went to the bridge and demanded command of the ship's communication system. His experience as a radar operator during World War II was evident as he radioed: "Rabaul: How do you read me?" he said. "Loud and clear!" came back the answer. The only explanation offered to us by the leading Russian scientists—that the captain's fear that one of his many disheartened fellow citizens on board would defect had been the trump card—was not satisfying to any of us even though it was plausible. But it was a product of the Soviet culture.

In amazement I watched the disparity: The international community of scientists, trained by their very discipline to be skeptical, to ask questions, and challenge the system, were remaining true to their inquisitive culture even under Soviet authority and, their energy turned into unruliness, reacting with upheaval in their demand for an honest explanation. In contrast, under the same circumstances, the Soviet community of scientists was squelching the same spirit of inquiry and challenge and demand for the truth they had learned and that they lived in their scientific practice. Where was the passion that allowed them to make on-board micron-scale-thin sections of rock with equipment encrusted by sea air? And the voices that debated strongly during seminars exacting rigorous answers or that chanted Georgian songs in nights of revelry? The energy was gone, replaced by disenchantment. It wasn't until later, back in Andy Bateman's cabin, that we understood the dichotomy as we thought about it in terms of Freudian psychology: we were watching the triumph of the survival instinct over values and culture. The culture of fear was the stronger of the two.

Create a Culture

TO EXCEL IN BREAKTHROUGH INNOVATION it is not enough to manage a group of talented individuals. It starts with survival of the culture, and to survive a leader must create a culture defined by beliefs, attitudes, energy, interaction style, and practices—and rituals. But to excel, the leader must ensure that the culture be one of creative engagement and liberating values. If it is clearly defined and rests on lived values, the group culture will flood the larger organization and, in so doing, create the network that is vital for innovation to take place. The effort needed is not defining a complex, multicomponent framework. Unlike top-to-bottom corporate efforts aimed at changing culture, which may take years to yield fruit, the creation of a culture within the intimacy of a single group allows effects to be quickly noticeable, and the dimensions that need to be addressed are basic ones.

At the core of a successful culture of innovation is the respect for the individual and the individual's freedom. The culture will develop as the leader provides the space for the emergence of the attitudes and practices that typify the group and provides the support for their survival. Well-established primitive cultures are the reflection of skills passed down from one generation to the next through oral traditions and rituals of celebration. In the same fashion, the value that a modern-day group with sophisticated innovation as its goal places on the same three pillars—time, sharing of knowledge through the oral tradition, and celebrations—leaves a defining imprint on the culture it creates.

The value placed on time defines the nature of a group. At the core of the creative process is a culture that creates negative space by eschewing frenetic habits and providing autonomy over time, thus enabling the flow of creative intuition. Sharing of knowledge through formal and informal exchanges allows identification and transmission of behaviors and accomplishments that are honored and deserving of emulation, and thus recognized and celebrated.

ESTABLISHING THE ORAL TRADITION

Whether in primitive cultures that rely on it or in sophisticated innovation settings, the oral tradition—that practice of sharing knowledge and cultural practices, wisdom and expectations, information and acceptable behavior, the know-how and the philosophy that permits the passing of the culture from one generation to the next—relies on two important elements: the physical setting for the sharing to take place and the nature of the get-togethers themselves.

CREATE SETTINGS THAT NURTURE KNOWLEDGE SHARING

The ability to collaborate and get along with others is paramount in enabling people to quickly share knowledge, either formally within a team or informally beyond the team. To foster informal knowledge transfer, teams need an environment that stimulates the senses and the emotions, one that fosters free association of ideas. An impassioned leader uses every lever, including workspaces and furnishings, to support the team culture. One effective way of promoting cross-pollination of ideas, actively coaching incoming talent, and keeping team members up to date is to establish "creativity rooms"—nicely decorated and furnished rooms that look more like living rooms, with comfortable leather couches and toys that encourage tinkering—where teams can drop in and use informally as needed. They are true "living" rooms, for it is here that the culture is lived. It is here that, along with knowledge and understanding, the sense of freedom that practitioners crave, once experienced, is shared and passed on as a cultural element, as discussed in the context of allowing space for wings to spread.

Only one rule should apply to a creativity room: it cannot be reserved for meetings, or it will become just one more conference room. It is to be used as the group sees fit: for one-on-one discussions, which might be joined by anybody else interested in the subject; to read an article, have lunch, or simply decompress; for coffee breaks and celebrations, and to brainstorm around a tough problem. It belongs to the group in which—it cannot be forgotten—you as a leader also participate. So it is important that you partake in the life that teems in the creativity room.

From Glass to Ceramics
Create Physical Space to Tinker

The first creativity room I set up was located on the fifth floor of the research building, where glass research is housed. Though he was not sure what I was up to, my director, Donald Jameson, was happy to let me go through with my unconventional suggestion. For years, Corning had tolerated scientists and technicians coming together and standing around lab benches for brief coffee breaks. But new government safety regulations banning food in laboratories would soon bring an end to this practice. The fifth floor was being renovated and I saw in that overhaul an opportunity to go from good to great.

Using a local interior decorator rather than the unaffordable corporate suppliers to procure leather couches and armchairs, coffee tables and side tables, and the scientists' choice for decorating the walls—framed scientific diagrams of phase equilibria rather than my choice of high-quality art—and with a small budget set aside for scientists, technicians, and administrators alike to purchase toys of their choosing to encourage mindless tinkering and carefree play, we created a space that in a short time would become the hub of the group. Twice a day informal, optional coffee breaks were held there that became the best way of staying current on world events, politics, the state of the lab, or the emotional temperature of the group. The requisite large whiteboard would often bear witness to the scientific discussion of the day. People would use it to keep track of predictions or challenges on technical accomplishments or the anticipated time for their delivery, even as an ongoing open, albeit nonproprietary, notebook to request insight and input. Some of the best research ideas were born out of discussions held there.

For me, as a leader, the creativity room represented not only a way of staying in touch with my people in an enjoyable, informal, and relaxed way and knowing where they stood on issues, but also a way of quickly polling them when I wanted their opinion and input. The legendary Mark Hewlett, the first person ever to make it to the rank of research fellow—the title had been actually created for him—was a highly creative scientist with one of the largest numbers of patents in the lab and somebody with broad interests in science, people, and the world. He and Brian MacHarg, the true-to-my-corduroys-and-my-esoteric-glasses scientist, could be considered the founding fathers of the coffee break and could almost invariably be relied on to be there leading the discussion. But in general people came and went, and not everybody was there all the time. Neither was I, though people knew they could find me there, and they would congregate there in search of information when there was exciting news or a difficult moment. That the presence of the leader has a binding force would be confirmed with the passage of time as Mark and Brian deplored the loss in vitality of their cherished coffee break tradition, wondering to what extent it was due to the infrequent presence of their leader at these habitual get-togethers.

Some of the members of the ceramics research group, housed in a different building, used to come up to the fifth floor to join in the daily coffee break conversations or participate in more organized activities. But it was not enough for them, and they would often ask for a creativity room closer to their surroundings. Their workspaces and furnishings constituted a source of mortification for me, as they did not reflect a spirit of celebration of their accomplishments and liberation of their creative talents. The contrast between the physical settings of the groups was stark, and I let them know that this in no way reflected their value or their contributions. When there were finally plans and funding to build a new facility for their part of the lab, we made sure a creativity room was included in the design of the area for ceramic research. Construction went only a bit further than the ceremony of the setting of the cornerstone before the hardship of the next recession reared up, bringing construction to a halt. But the culture had been firmly established, and the scientists did not give in on their request. In time, as I returned to Corning after three years in France, Narendra Ambani, one of the ceramics scientists who for years had frequented the fifth-floor creativity room, made a point of coming by my office to escort me to an undisclosed location. The destination turned out to be a creativity room for the ceramics research group, with leather chairs and framed photographs on the wall and whiteboard and all. One of his recent original oil paintings sat at an easel. And he described the same kind of activities and life and spirit that creativity rooms engender. He was proud of their room. I was proud of them all.

ENCOURAGE FORUMS THAT ADVANCE KNOWLEDGE SHARING

For teams chartered with delivering breakthroughs that can change the world, sharing knowledge takes many forms beyond the formal, the informal, or the casual. The complexity of most fields today has grown beyond the reaches of a single discipline, and the best ideas come from multidisciplinary fields of expertise. Sure, a large organization will have many formal project reviews, business technology poster sessions, tutorials, and guest lecturers, all designed to disseminate information on a large scale. But these rarely satisfy the need to take the incisive look that only a group of experts can offer, or the intimate atmosphere where learning can become an unencumbered mental stretching exercise. And so the extra need to share results, to seek input, to gain insight, inspires activities that are an expression of the interest and mission of the group. Whether formally or informally, having your experts train and coach each other is not only expansive for them and for you as leader—as mentioned already from the perspective of giving them the space to enlarge their influence—but it plays a major role in passing down acquired knowledge and, therefore, in creating an enduring culture.

The Glass Nucleus
Cultivate Enriching Long-Term Traditions

The scientists of the glass research group organized an internal forum that they aptly named the "Glass Nucleus" to discuss subjects of interest to them. They had few rules, but the rules were specific and the members were particular in enforcing them. The forum was scheduled and attended only by technical personnel; managers were not invited, though there were few and rare exceptions. Attendees were welcome to suggest topics for discussion and to enlist themselves or others as presenters. Otherwise the organizer was at liberty to choose a topic and a presenter. Presentations were to be informal, with preparation requiring a minimum of effort. Simple notes scribbled on overhead sheets were favored, and slides, PowerPoint, or other fancy presentations were shunned. The forum proved to have the longevity that accompanies success. It would occasionally slow down as a function of the energy of the organizer, Peter Murray proving to be by far the most energetic and successful of them, which resulted in his enjoying no term limits. As a group leader my role was to provide the budget for coffee and doughnuts and otherwise stand by. I would occasionally suggest topics or encourage them to invite a speaker, but only occasionally. This was how plant engineers from the U.S. single-mode fiber plant came to solicit help for their contamination issue that had been plaguing them for more than six months, the same problem that took Dave Johnson a week to solve and three weeks to implement the solution. Over the years, ideas were spurred, scientific principles debated, solutions argued, results delivered. And, just as significantly for the participants, a sense of self-determination, of autonomy, of empowerment, was experienced by all, as a liberating and creative force was passed down from one generation of practitioners to the next.

Intimate Tutorials
Enable Short-Lived Practices

In the early stage of Corning's entrance into the photonics market, when core technology managers debated hotly whether we should cease to be a materials-based company and become instead an optical systems company, all material researchers felt their very presence questioned. There were many opportunities for the development of new materials—for purposes such as the transmission of signals at different wavelengths, their amplification, or their switching—and the researchers' minds were well trained to develop materials for specific requirements. *Any* required property, whether thermal or mechanical or optical, can be addressed this way. Optical physicists, however, were used to designing modules and equipment *only* with existing materials. It was time for retrenching and regrouping. In this case, I spearheaded the effort, and the glass research group organized a series of tutorials—"Intimate Tutorials" we called them—that would allow the two sides, the world of physical requirements and the world of material options, to face each other. The premise was simple: basic optical physics, meet sophisticated material phase stability. The setting was simple as well: a non-threatening, all-questions-welcome atmosphere led by our own physicists and material scientists. With subjects chosen by our group, we would retreat for an afternoon to a location away from the research lab where we would not face interruptions. After some months of learning and exploring, of growing and expanding, we no longer felt the need for this propping-up of concepts and options. Having served us right, the "Intimate Tutorials" came to a close.

As support for a culture is made tangible, that culture will emerge, with its own beliefs, attitudes, energy, interaction style, and practices. This need not take years. The creation of a culture within the intimacy of a group has effects that are quickly noticeable: sharing of knowledge through formal and informal exchanges allows easy identification and transmission of the defining elements of the culture. If the group culture is clearly defined and supported by lived values, it will flood the larger organization, creating a vital network of innovation. It is a most rewarding experience to see this practice at work, the power of culture passed down through the years. A decade after leaving the directorship of the inorganic technologies group, I was made aware of the power of the survival of culture as Tim Cobb, physicist, ballroom dancer, and now culture promoter, who understood that there is no need to wait for official sanctioning of activities to reinforce the value and richness of oral tradition, shared with excitement his new goings-on.

The Society Committed to Relaxation

Create and Establish a Culture and It Will Prevail

Having discovered his other self through the process that released the dancer in the physicist and unleashed the gregarious in the loner, and after many years of working with others and mentoring the younger, Tim Cobb felt the urge to again explore the area of compaction of glass that had pulled him away from fundamental physics. By pulling together like-minded scientists from different departments, he started a discussion group in search of an answer to one specific question: "How can we make a better compaction model?"—a question that led them to the broader issues of glass relaxation and onto glass processing. The notion was to meet in the creativity room and create a space where all could bring ideas. No speakers were to be designated, but many contributors would be expected to participate and influence each other. The result has been the creation of the Society Committed to Relaxation (of Glass!!), a vibrant group of eight to fifteen people that meets weekly in what has become every participant's favorite meeting; nobody wants to leave once the two hours are up. Tim, who leads the meetings and sends a weekly agenda in advance, has a unique combination of passion for what he does and calm demeanor in expressing his views that has undoubtedly created a spirit of respect, and the meetings have become not only a place where all can bring new ideas, but a forum where all can expect their contributions to be counted, discussed, and built on, a forum where everybody feels respected, even embraced. The tone of openness and forthrightness was originally set by a few outspoken people—the likes of the forceful Peter Murray, who personifies the hot fire of creativity, and the younger Ben Pulanski, with his strong fundamental background from Stanford—who knew and trusted each other and set the tone with their joking and friendly atmosphere, which allowed quieter or younger people to feel more relaxed and open up. As facilitator, Tim has always made it his responsibility to "protect" anyone from being silenced—while allowing for the interruptions needed for a lively discussion—by returning to speakers who might have been eclipsed by another. Veteran researchers and retirees who join in, with their love for respectful disagreements, make modeling this behavior an easy walk.

Thus the society grew organically into what it is. And it has gone beyond being a feel-good organization, or one of the few places where scientists can still do just basic science, to an organization that delivers tangible results. In its first year, the group had an impact on five different projects, including the process to deliver the cover glass that protects the best smartphones of the twenty-first century. And they continue to look for relaxation issues of all sorts in projects throughout the lab. Their only risk appears to be that their success increase their numbers beyond the capacity of the creativity room. But their response to that has already been defined: for them, it is clear that doing this in an auditorium would cause it to fail. So they would rather sit on the floor if it gets too crowded in the creativity room than move the meeting anywhere else.

Who says that a thorny subject such as the relaxation of glass cannot be relaxing for the mind and body? Just give it the space to flourish and the respect to thrive, and you will have the best of oral tradition practices, those needed for the survival of a culture. For the activity has gone beyond creating a forum for discussion: it is allowing space for others to fly, embracing creative conflict, demanding excellence, and enriching lives. In short, it is living the passions of innovation.

As leaders, it is immeasurably valuable to learn to feel at ease with the concept that less is more, with the idea that there are times when managers are not needed. The healthy growth of oral traditions is one of them. So feel composed in encouraging groups to meet on their own, without leaders or managers present, on a regular basis of their choice. Furthermore, create the culture that gives them the space to emerge *on their own*. Resist the urge to continually analyze and schedule, but be prepared to respond when you identify a need. And you will be surprised as you see a sense of empowerment arising that liberates creativity and persists over time.

SIGNIFICANCE IN RECOGNITION

To be coherent and lasting, a culture relies on open communication and recognition to build the trust that delivers high performance. There is a certain Darwinian principle that applies to the power of recognition in maintaining a culture: appreciating, recognizing, and rewarding each other's contributions are ways of pointing out desirable behaviors, those selected for emulation. So in addition to being important motivating forces for individuals—particularly in breakthrough innovation, where the number of failures far outweighs the number of successes—reward and recognition are also important culture-building forces for the group.

Unfortunately, in an understandable desire to protect privacy and discourage dissent and jealousy, most forms of "big" rewards—cash awards, merit increases, bonuses, stock options—need to be kept private, and so their value in promoting desirable behavior and performance is lost to the group. With their outstanding potential for motivation, they are nevertheless important forms of recognition, one that leaders should make every effort to use as frequently and generously as possible.

PROMOTIONS: SOMETHING TO TAKE DEAD SERIOUSLY

On the other end of the spectrum lies the promotion, the public nature of which represents an important force in motivation and culture creation. A significant part of the impact of promotions on culture comes from the fact that promotions are the return on accountability—the reward for the accountability trusted upon the receiver—informing the group what contributions and behaviors are of preeminent importance. But in order for them to be a creative rather than a destructive force, promotions need to be judged and awarded with the greatest sense of fairness. Promote for the right reasons and you have the wind behind you. Promote for misguided reasons—the pressure to retain a star, an effort to support diversity, or a well-intentioned attempt at leveling the playing field—and you run into gale winds of resistance and backlash. Though promotion recommendations are not public documents, the behaviors and accomplishments that have earned them, as part of the ethos of the group, are indeed public and have been recognized by the community all along. When deserved, the reward of the promotion will consolidate the figure to be emulated. If not, it will become a mockery. Needless to say, specific technical contributions, enabling capabilities, ideas, and advances all constitute the core of the achievements required for promotion and should be easy for a leader to identify. But alongside these, and completing the package, there need to be behaviors and attitudes that make the contributor deserving of promotion. And it is in recognizing these two contrasting dimensions, the technical and the human—the yin and the yang of the social process that is innovation and that can be made or broken by human dynamics—that a leader finds his best opportunity to define and consolidate the culture that he is working to create.

Identifying and endorsing candidates for promotion is both a serious responsibility and a rewarding experience for leaders, as the exercise brings forth the tangible impact of some of our most meaningful efforts on behalf of others. As leaders, we deliver results through developing people and honoring individuality while providing structure and guidance. And we encourage risk taking, experimentation, and diversity of ideas as well as cross-disciplinary thinking and knowledge transfer, key characteristics to look for in assessing people's growth and evaluating their promotion potential. It is our responsibility as leaders to consider promotions with the greatest of care and pride as they, in a nutshell, define what the group stands for. So look at the contributions and, alongside the growth of the human being, look for balanced human equations such as:

The Yin and the Yang
Recognize the Human as Much as the Delivery

- The ability to bring significant technical impact to bear over an enlarging sphere of influence *coupled with* an interest in mentoring younger scientists and technicians and the desire to collaborate with other established scientists

- The pairing of a fertile and creative mind with the ability to demonstrate early-stage concepts with simple tools *coupled with* the eagerness to participate in projects that create a community

- The ability to drive teams from a technical perspective *coupled with* a supportive and compassionate side that knows no boundaries, that reaches out, high and low, to those who need it

- A position as a world-class exploratory researcher who has placed the organization in a leadership position, *coupled with* intellectual honesty, rigor, and a frankness that keeps you and your group on your toes

- The bringing together of the creativity that typifies the exploratory scientist with the rigor of the engineer *coupled with* a drive that stems from inquisitiveness, not from the search for glory

- Not being afraid of stepping ahead of the curve technically *coupled with* being a solid human being, deeply rooted in values, with the tolerance forged by the blending of the experience of many cultures

MORE THAN INFORMAL: STRENGTHEN THE CULTURE THROUGH RECOGNITION

In addition to formal recognition, most organizations encourage and use different forms of informal recognition: movie tickets, gift certificates, even time off. These also play an important role in motivation and strengthening culture, and they become much more effective if they are customized by you for your group. Just the fact that it is tailored to them individually, rather than included on the latest list of "how to keep your group motivated and on its toes," moves it up several notches in appreciation value.

Make It a Date
Tailor Your Gestures of Appreciation

Corning the corporation is headquartered in Corning the town, with a population well under ten thousand (fifteen thousand for the larger "metropolitan" area). The number of restaurants in town, reflective of its population, is artificially large only because of the needs of it largest employer. Just a few weeks is all it takes for the town's residents to become familiar with the menus in most establishments. During the summer, to everybody's delight, the options for gourmet dining expand significantly as a result of the seasonal opening of eateries that dot the nearby Finger Lakes. Within a forty-five-minute drive you can enjoy a fine French or Eastern European or Continental menu while sipping good wine and watching one of the lakes below you. This situation inspired me to come up with a way to recognize contributions or behavior that could easily fall through the cracks of the recognition spectrum: too meaningful for a small, informal recognition certificate, not quite deserving of a large cash award. For these cases my administrative assistant would make fancy certificates with an inspired design, "Entitling the bearer and an accompanying guest to dinner at the restaurant of their choice." I would give little guidance beyond insisting that it should feel like a celebration and not merely a way of avoiding the chore of cooking dinner. The details of restaurant choice, wine, and other things were left for the recipient to judge, guided only by corporate economic circumstances, the significance of their accomplishment, and their integrity. That it was tailored to their likes and taste and that there was an element of trust in the recipients made it an incredibly popular and well-received form of recognition. And one incredibly simple to both personalize and handle, to boot. All that was needed was my signature on the expense report.

IN A CLASS BY ITSELF: RECOGNIZE MASTERY

Then there is a form of recognition that is subtle and has a pervasive and lasting effect on culture: the recognition of mastery—the *daily* recognition of mastery. The leader who expects the members of her group to become the best they can be will be wise to recognize their steps in getting there and, by so doing, help the group move toward achieving mastery, the merging of professional excellence and personal fulfillment.

Recognition of mastery has many faces and presents opportunities on a daily basis, most of them taking place in the intimacy of the group. On these two qualities, intimacy and constancy, rests the all-encompassing impact that recognition of mastery delivers, a sustained effect in shaping culture through honest, reiterated communication and celebration.

When carried out in a *timely* fashion and delivered with sincerity and a personal message, small actions of recognition are the daily nourishment that recognizes influence and impact and helps those being recognized feel established as practitioners. Opportunities that have impact are easy to find:

Little Gestures for Big Masters

Be Thoughtful in Finding Occasions Daily

- Asking everyone to share what *they* consider their most significant highlight of the month at the group meeting; it is likely that this will be the exploratory one that does not make it into your selection of highlights for your own boss

- Endorsing their initiative for their own forum or discussion group—and sending in the doughnuts

- Bringing by a relevant high-level executive to an office or lab for an unexpected *private* pat on the back

- Assigning a second technician to a productive scientist whose overload has forced her to work as one herself

- Making a mention at your group meeting of a recent external honor awarded to one of them

- Asking seasoned scientists to mentor younger ones

- Assigning resources to parlay the outcome of one project into a broader impact

- Inviting expressions of appreciation and reward by team members for one another's contributions.

Opportunities for small acts of recognition abound in the day of a leader. So be eager to detect the face of anticipation at the delivery of a result, the sign of satisfaction in the discussion of a new possibility, the joy in the recent promotion. And, simply, share them with the rest of the group in a way that it touches lives.

CELEBRATIONS: EVERY EFFORT TO TAILOR THEM PAYS OFF

Celebrations are one other form of expressing appreciation, also one with strong impact on culture creation. Like other aspects of recognition, celebrations need not be cumbersome or dull. Whether personal—marking a promotion, an award, a birthday, or a wedding shower—or focused on team successes or corporate events, as discussed in the passage on the value of fun and play, what makes these occasions enjoyable and memorable is the thoughtfulness that goes into making them personal and meaningful instead of extravagant and canned. Their capacity for swaying culture resides in their very nature: they allow for up-close interaction and encourage people to "bring out the child" to the sound of conversation and music, an unconstrained display of the social behavior of your group. So, as a leader, find meaningful opportunities for celebration, plan them with attention to detail, and enjoy the opportunity they bring to have fun surrounded by people that mean a lot to you.

THE VALUE OF TIME

A third important element of culture is time, or, rather, the value that is given to time as a tool for exploration and discussion. The value placed on time is a core element that so clearly defines the very nature of a culture that it can be sensed when you are part of a group. Time that is chopped up into bits and segments is experienced as feverish activity and confusion, and it is not productive time. But most significantly, it has a harsh impact on the creative process. Have you ever tried to force the flow of creative juices, whether in writing or in designing with blocks and colors or in thinking of a new life-saving surgical procedure into the forty-five minutes between meetings? Or to work around the clock to deliver something new—not just to make calculations or put the presentation together or do the typing, but to *create* something new—by putting in ten hours a day several days in a row? The experienced inventive mind knows the answer very well: It just does not work that way. You feel either rushed or exhausted, and the ideas do not flow.

It is common knowledge that the best ideas come when you least expect them—in the shower, during a nature walk, in the drowsiness of dawn, even in dreams. The answer you need flows when the uncluttered mind has the space that allows it to arrive. It is then that you have access to the sharp insights, the intuition, that hard-to-explain immediate knowing that does not need to rely on rational or logical processes. Ideas and the passion behind them need uncluttered time to flow, and the leader should therefore allow for "negative space," time for passion to flourish and ideas to break free. To understand this is to know the essence of the creative process. A frenetic work pace allows time only for today's pressing tasks. But creativity is inversely related to the number of tasks being worked on. The leader must actively clear clutter and distraction and push scientists to eschew frenetic work habits and overwork. Ask yourself: Do practitioners really need to attend all those meetings? Is it really important for them to fill out time sheets? How frequently does upper management need progress reports? The answers are obvious and the solutions simple, though they may require a shifting of habits. Most importantly, the shift in habits requires that you, the leader, be relentless in defending the time of your team and in not overscheduling their days; not every scientist is needed at every meeting when one team representative will do. And do not attempt to keep track of what they do and when they do it. Assigned time is enough for accounting; more spaced short highlights, rather than frequent long reports, better meet the requirements of upper management.

Cultures differ in the value they place on time for creation. The idea that "negative space" is creative and valuable time is not shared by all cultures. Groups that have been expected to value busy-ness and the frenzy of constant activity are conditioned by their leader to stay in that high-intensity mode and may have difficulty shifting gears.

Old Imprints Don't Fade Fast
Above All, Support the Culture

Not long after I arrived to run Corning's technology group in France, many started requesting a creativity room of their own. Their familiarity with the fifth-floor facility back in the United States made this a priority on their list, one could say their expectation of me. It was easy for me to be receptive, of course, and I asked for a team of volunteers to find and suggest potential sites and a second team to make recommendations on furnishings and decorations. The resulting effort maintained some familiar elements— leather couches, coffee tables—while adding that uniquely French sense of style in shapes and colors. Two new elements made the room stand out.

The first, a large aquarium that the community at large had only dreamed and longed for, became a center of attention for the lab personnel, who would take as much enjoyment in feeding the fish as in keeping track of newborns in a way that made you think they were their own. More than a decorative or ice-breaking piece, the aquarium became a symbolic element, with bubble making by the fish representing idea generation; their coalescence the coming together of notions; and their growth the eventual definition as projects. Truly an inspirational piece.

The second element came at the initiative of François Sunik, the multitalented renaissance man, who volunteered to make a connection with the arts center in his hometown to let us hang original art from their exhibits once the shows closed. With time, his persistence enabled us to enjoy original works by many contemporary French artists, exposing the technical and administrative communities to new styles, some of them raising passionate controversies among our own "art critics."

I started using the creativity room for activities such as birthday celebrations and community gatherings. It was becoming "lived in." I could tell, though, that the assembled group would disperse quickly after an event; I did not see the usual lingering and exchanging and engaging in carefree conversation of other creativity rooms. Eventually, I realized that the room was unused for most of the day. I would see occasionally a visitor being greeted there, or even meeting with our people. But there were no regular coffee breaks or simply people who dropped in to take a break, let alone peers venting and discussing. I made an effort to go there myself, but most of the time I would find it empty or with a casual passerby. My inquiries and conversations with senior scientists disclosed an unexpected reaction: they and their colleagues were hesitant to just drop by because it would give the impression of being unproductive, of wasting time—not an impression that anybody wanted their peers, let alone their supervisors, to have. It was clear to me at that point that there was still much more work to do in creating a culture.

In the same way the conductor sets the pace that makes music or cacophony, the values, expectations, and modeling behavior of the leader provides the value that the group places on time. So as a leader do not shy away from time outside your office, when you wander off into offices and labs with no more specific purpose than to find out, "What's up?" and "What does it feel like?" Do not stay away from the break area or creativity room, and don't be in a hurry every time you show up. Schedule time for carefree celebrations. And remind them, time and again, that productivity does not come from frenetic activity. It comes from listening to the flow of your intuition—or risk losing it—and from having the freedom and responsibility to choose the right activity for the moment.

A CULTURE NEEDS A LEADER: TO YOUR OWN SELF BE TRUE

The culminating aspect of culture is clearly the leader, or, rather, the space the leader needs to find for himself, the space to develop a management style that is true to the culture of liberating values he is creating. An impassioned symphonic orchestra needs a conductor in kind, a true, honest, passionate conductor that resonates with the players in a genuine way. It is not reasonable to ask a leader to create a culture of liberating values by giving prescriptive values and principles that confine and limit him and do not allow for the liberation of his own true values. Leaders need to be true to their own selves, and it is only through unleashing their own style that they will be successful in unleashing their groups.

It is important for leaders who work at creating healthy organizations and motivating people to take charge of their satisfaction and high performance at work *while simultaneously* being true to themselves and making their own work meaningful and satisfying. The role of the leader demands that you stand on firm ground and achieve the balance that only being true to your nature can provide. So be true to yourself as you create the leadership style and culture that are true to you, and liberate your values to find the style that resonates with you and allows you to create your own unique culture.

Make It Your Own

Know Yourself and Let Your Actions Resonate with You

From my experience I can speak for some of the things that are second nature to me and that have resulted in creating the style and culture that are true to me. I believe that it is essential to:

- Find the way of tapping people's talent, developing new skills, broadening people's experiences. Creatives are driven to deliver—it is the nature of their work. Sometimes they just need a bit of space, some encouragement, a little direction.

- Be hands-on in providing guidance, coaching, and judgment about priorities but always remember the "art of nonmanagement": the only one that works with highly intelligent, creative workers who are trained to be skeptical and to challenge the system and who don't have much use for bosses.

- Balance assignments to make sure that talent doesn't languish and that people are attacking organizational priorities. Always keep in mind that perhaps the single most important thing that prevents success is assigning people to the wrong projects and asking them to play roles that are at odds with their individual strengths.

- Ask those in your group often how they are doing and how they are feeling, and don't be afraid to open up views of them that you had never seen. Just be honest with them; they are too smart for sugarcoating.

- Manage one by one: one person at a time, one project at a time, one situation at a time.

- Foster a personal, open dynamic that intentionally blurs hierarchical distinctions.

- Honor and respect those in your group—and all others as well—as individuals.

- Adapt your management style to the individual, becoming more like an individual's private coach or personal developer than a boss. Understand what kind of work environment suits which individual, under what circumstances the individual is motivated or not motivated, and what hidden strengths need to be developed.

- Have as a goal to help people feel so good about themselves that they don't need to punch someone else in order to attain that feeling.

- And keep reminding yourself—and them too: they work with you, not for you. Your true role is to *serve them.*

These beliefs and behaviors resonate with me and aid me in creating cultures. And so I encourage *you* as leader to liberate *your* values to find the style that resonates with *you* and that will allow you to unleash a culture that can create, innovate, and deliver while at the same time unleashing your own self. All eyes are on you as leader. Your level of comfort with who you are, your self-assurance and your hesitation, your very style, are all evident to your group and the organization at large. So dig deeply in understanding who you are, become aware of your conditioning, your reactions, your values. And let these guide your values and the style in leading your group and in interacting with the larger organization. They will then resonate with you, echo the comfort that you find in yourself, and find it second nature in them to follow you.

An Urgency for Structure

ALMOST OVERNIGHT the technology group grew from five core technologies to nineteen, from being materials-centric to having a lack of focus. Acrid discussions ensued among the nineteen core technology directors—with an eighteen-to-one ratio of males to females—that now shared the table, with the newcomers asserting, with a hostility and style in sharp contrast to the polite corporate culture that defines Corning, that the corporation should become an optical systems company and that materials were "passé" in a photonics era. Maintaining a clear sense of strategy and priorities was hindered by the reporting structure: the nineteen directors no longer reported to a single research director, who could define a clear direction and make decisions, but to three codirectors of research. Making things more difficult, not all three research directors had the technical backgrounds and experience desired to lead the technology groups under them. But enveloping it all was the lack of understanding of the overarching organizational structure—who was responsible for what, what the ties were between the groups and their people, who was in leading and supporting roles—that added to the chaotic feeling of this already confusing stage of hypergrowth.

The lab felt uncertain and the flow of work was difficult. For us, the leadership of the research competency groups, the silver lining was to be found amidst the confusion, because in a way it gave us the leeway to put our own imprint on the organization and in so doing to grow as leaders. These were both trying times and growth times for all, and whereas most of us had different preoccupations driven by the uniqueness of each group—its strength, position inside a fluid company, ability to deliver, even survivability—there was one thing that could bring us all together, and that was the question of how to coordinate execution and delivery. The answer, some would argue, rested on the clear definition, acceptance, and execution of roles, links, and responsibilities. We all agreed that it needed to be worked on, but, daunted by the sheer magnitude of the effort, few volunteered.

No one led the charge more fervently than Dan Blair, a seasoned manager who had risen within the telecommunications organization. He had a sharp intellect and a broad capacity for abstract thinking coupled with an appetite for debate punctuated by sharp humor and a sometimes deadly sting. Through years of sharing family meals with him and his wife Nora where we addressed every subject from world travel and politics to the care of elderly parents or the life of veterinary medicine that our daughters shared, I had learned to appreciate his sharpness in thought and word and to enjoy the give-and-take. I was happy to have his leadership on this endeavor.

It was a demanding exercise that a small group of us undertook with the support and expectation of the rest. With meticulous detail, we outlined positions and chains of command, and, from top to bottom and for every single role in an organization with dozens of directors, we discussed and defined scope and focus, budget responsibilities and decisions on allocations, chairing responsibility and frequency of meetings, reporting relationship and advisory responsibilities, customers, and direct reports. We cross-checked for consistency and eliminated roundabouts, loopholes, and duplications.

In an iterative process, with progress reported back to the larger group and feedback incorporated into our proposal, we refined our thinking and moved toward a deliverable. Rather than a dictum that would propel us overnight into optimum levels of organizational efficiency, the goal was to create among us enough understanding of the need for organizational clarity to allow each one of us to impact our own groups and all of us to abide by the same definitions and practices.

It worked for many of us, each one benefiting from it as a function of his own drive. For those of us around the discussion table late into the night after an already long day, the payoff came from living a culture of rich argument and rigorous debate, from challenging assumptions, poking fun at comebacks, occasionally even driving each other to our limits, but ultimately from learning about the need for clear organization and its ability to make or break the mission of a group.

Structure a Clear Organization

ADDRESSING THE DIFFICULT TECHNOLOGY CHALLENGES that we face today requires disciplined teams working within clearly defined organizational structures. To deliver technology, creative teams benefit—and know enough to request—organizational structure. The complexity of the process demands it, the teams need it, and individual scientists thrive within it. No, it is not contradictory to encourage scientists to use both the right and left sides of their brains, to be more intuitive, to follow their inner drive, while recognizing the need for a well-defined organization. A clearly defined organization, in which every player understands her role in making technology delivery happen, does precisely what the creative mind craves: it eliminates barriers.

STRUCTURE? WHY?

By defining a clear organization, the stumbling blocks—second-guessing, the fear that "it can't be done," risk-averse knee-jerk reactions, circuitous approval paths, and many other pitfalls—are eliminated and replaced by a streamlined delivery process. The time invested in defining a structure, with roles, links, and responsibilities clearly understood by all, is time well spent. And consistently defining and revisiting these three parameters need not be exercises of high complexity, merely of high clarity. Neither should it be an exercise in the segregation of practices. The need to focus on clear organizational structure in no way demands a turning-away from maintaining the vibrancy of an organization, of establishing values, demanding excellence, and creating a culture by taking care of your team members one at a time. Just the opposite: both need to coexist with equal intensity, enthusiasm, and rigor.

Creatives Clamor for It
Insist on Definition and Support Them

Though the effect of organizational clarity on the creative mind is often dismissed, it impacts the practitioners' day-to-day activity and anima, and nobody can express this yearning for organizational clarity better than the innovation practitioners themselves:

- "It [organizational clarity] translates to a freedom, knowing who has responsibility for what. Just clearly knowing it. You can go about things and when you need something, get a resource, have a problem, it is clear who the leader is and you can go and talk to that person."

- "This [understanding of the organization] links directly to knowing who the leader is: the leader is in the loop, knows who is making the contributions. Lack of this is a disincentive."

- "The idea that we are going to participate in [poorly structured] projects like this is belittling. We need to find a balance between the freedom to share ideas and the fear of not getting credit. Credit is not the most important thing in the long run, but you do want to have the feeling that your work is being recognized."

- "That's the key: managers who know their role and their resources and have good connections to each other to link people up so we can work."

A structure, however, needs to strike a balance between two organizational extremes. On one hand, authoritarian hierarchies impose great clarity on an organization or team but they can also stifle creativity and passionate exploration. Free-form organizations, on the other hand, provide no boundaries or guidance for unconventional spirits, who often flounder without the structure imposed by a more traditional organization. The need, then, is for a clearly defined *impassioned* organization where everybody's role and everybody's responsibility is clear to all and where every exchange reinforces the role of each component.

Oddly enough, a clearly defined organization provides freedom rather than restriction. The more comfortable every member is in understanding his own role, the less he will feel driven to engage defense mechanisms to defend his turf. It is this absence of destructive conflict that creates space and liberates passions. Free-form organizations, by contrast, with their poor definition of roles, responsibilities, and space, and with bouncing links that rely on one aspect of a relationship today and on another tomorrow, elicit those feelings of insecurity and resulting turf battles that destroy the sense of freedom. In the progression from creative research to development and manufacturing, the need is for the coexistence of the organic organizational structures that Burns and Stalker defined half a century ago in their contingency theory for dynamic, uncertain environments and their mechanistic ones for stable environments.

WHO HAS THE SKILLS TO DO WHAT AND WITH WHOM?

At the core of any organization are, naturally, the practitioners. Any effort to provide them with clear and simple pathways of information and direction, of responsibilities and connections that transcend hierarchical barriers, will travel with ripple-effect magnification to outlying organizational circles—as will the loss of productivity that results from ignoring them.

The spirit established by the respect for clearly defined roles and by the understanding and implementation of responsibilities provides each player clarity regarding his own role and responsibilities and the assurance that his space will not be encroached upon, his role will be respected, his opinions heard, and his decisions not second-guessed—in sharp contrast to the behaviors of fighting for turf, elbowing your way in, demanding respect for ideas, and recognition for results, which are common to freewheeling organizations. This holds true at all levels of the organization, and observing it consolidates the leadership team in its position as strategy and decision makers while creating the spirit of trust that enables ideas and inventions to move freely within and across organizations. In turn, this spirit of clarity and respect lends muscle and flexibility to the organization as it enhances its ability to coordinate delivery and execution.

From the perspective of the individual, there are two basic questions, the answers to which streamline work and facilitate delivery: "Who takes care of my personal needs?" and "Who takes care of my project needs?" The answer, of course, defines a basic and fundamental distinction in roles and responsibilities, one that is not always identified or addressed by organizations, creating unnecessary confusion and holding back progress. And the answer is as simple as defining and differentiating two roles: functional and project management.

Taking care of defining assignments, of developing careers, and maintaining motivation and challenge is the purview of functional managers. These are the people to whom practitioners turn for direction, for arbitration, for support. In a complementary role, taking responsibility for enlisting the best resources for a project, defining the timelines, and driving team members to deliver on goals and schedules is the domain of project managers. These are the people to whom practitioners turn for clarity in project objectives, access to resources, and timeline definition.

In an organization, the need for definition and differentiation between these two roles—functional manager and project manager—cannot be stressed too much: practitioners need clarity, the organization benefits from it, results demand it. And neither can the need to understand the contrast in skills, personalities, and interests called for by the two different roles: people orientation, competency focus, long-term view, culture creation for the functional manager; hard drive, goal focus, short-term view, detail orientation for the project manager. From the perspective of the innovation practitioner, the difference can be summed up simply: A functional manager is somebody of whom his direct reports should say, "He is *so good* to work with," whereas a project manager is somebody of whom project team members should say, "She is *so tough* to work with." Differ as they may, both are essential in delivering excellence and should be able to complement each other in doing so. In successful partnerships both functional and project managers understand and respect each other's role and live the relationship by honoring their interdependence, with full recognition that the success of their near-term endeavor—and that of future endeavors that will rest on the survival of their long-term relationship—depends on their mutual reliance and collaboration.

It is all too natural in organizations that rely on technology—or other highly specialized fields, whether in health care or the arts—to also rely on their best technical performers for leadership, on the assumption that she who is good at one will also be good at the other. High potential is often first observed through the delivery of science and technology, and opportunities for growth are identified as a result. And this, the key step in the development of a person and a career, often lacks the subtlety needed for success: awareness of the interests, drive, and passion behind the performance. With the best intentions, practitioners are offered interesting challenges with a perspective that looks more forward than inward. And so for the high-potential candidate unaware of himself, the pull of an enticing career can be confusing and hard to resist, particularly the allure of the misguided concept of power in management positions—for only with time do most leaders come to the realization that power does not come with a position; it comes from those we serve, the people in our organizations.

As leaders we are in an exceptional position of touching people's lives, and we have a unique opportunity to do so in ways that support them in their growth, develop them in their careers, and bring out the best in them. In practice, every time a leader assigns somebody a role or simply asks them to fulfill a task, he is living this role of service and would be well advised to remind himself that if he does one thing right—getting the right person in the right role—everything falls into place. At times this can be straightforward and clear from the beginning. At other times it brings on the pain of broken dreams before awareness brings clarity. The latter was the case with Sebastian Estephe.

Finding His Calling
Serve Creatives by Coaxing Them

When Sebastian first started reporting to me he was already the manager of one of the inorganic materials research groups. His life experience had been shaped by duality: a background in chemistry and in material science, an education in East and West Coast establishments, an experience in the interplay between energy and solid materials, an interest in technology and in marketing. He was comfortable straddling fences, at times not even aware that he was unique in doing so.

A fifteen-year veteran in the technology group, he had earned the credibility of the organization by delivering a wide variety of materials and devices addressing chemical, electrical, and related needs. In a way unlike anybody else, he brought together the fundamental understanding of solid materials and an ability to conceptualize applications and materialize devices from his new materials. Later training in technology marketing and product innovation only sharpened his position and potential.

For some time before taking on his current responsibility, Sebastian's identification as successor to his functional manager had been shaping his own self-image. He continued to put in an outstanding technical performance, growing from his early generation of ideas and simple devices to eventually addressing major societal and industry needs in energy generation with complex systems designed around novel material inventions, and demonstrating remarkable effectiveness in establishing a team and moving projects downstream. To the outsider it was clear that he had all the makings of a superior project manager. In his own internal dialogue, however, he could not escape the indelible image of functional manager that had been projected on him.

In being given responsibility for the functional group, Sebastian not only received internal gratification but external recognition, at times a treacherous advisor for personal growth. As I started guiding him it was easier for me than it was for him to read what was at the core of his lack of drive for mentoring his young scientists and for supporting and setting free mature ones. This became easier to understand when contrasted with his passion for delineating new programs and developing technical targets: we had a project manager at heart dressed in the robes of a functional manager, and the lack of vibrancy in his group was the clear evidence. He was leading one major program with external partners and funding, while having functional responsibility for a competency group. He was comfortable having one leg on each side and could not tell what was energizing from what was draining him.

There is an apparent contradiction to the role of the leader in that it is easier to use authority and influence to tighten up and make people cautious than to use them to open up and make people more courageous. When the stakes are high and the consequences serious, as leaders we need the willingness to be accountable for the well-being of the larger organization and operate in service, rather than in control, of those around us.

The solution to the situation was clear: Sebastian was the ideal person to become the official project manager of the effort he was leading, and we had already identified other candidates with strong functional management skills who could easily run Sebastian's group. He knew about this option and did not find it compelling, but in my mind neither was the choice of a forced move. In my aim of delivering technology through developing people, I had learned from Dasa about the profundity of awareness and about the power of supporting people to be aware. "Awareness gives people freedom, power, and choice, strengthening their ability to change," he would remind us. Sebastian presented me with one of my greatest challenges in this endeavor. Intense sessions of mentoring feedback—to which Sebastian brought listening and paying attention and I offered gentle but relenting inquiry—provided him with clear sight into his nature and behavior, his inner drive versus his sense of responsibility, and his public persona. In the end he could see how his lack of awareness was leading him to desire a role contrary to his energy, skills and drive. With awareness, he gained the clarity and the courage to choose. The struggle was over.

Sebastian went on to experience that liberating joy of bringing together vocation and avocation, for his bringing together of skills in fundamental understanding, market judgment, and project leadership positioned him exceptionally well to deliver in early-stage growth opportunities. He said little, for he is not the boisterous type, but there was no need, for we could all read his energy, his drive, his smile. I received his subtle message as I opened the bestselling book we had once discussed and that he had wrapped and left on my desk with a single word on it. "Thanks," it read.

Sebastian continued to evolve as a human being, growing in skills and abilities, and addressing challenges in his professional and personal life. Fortunately for all, he never lost that energy and that smile that made it clear that he knew well who he was.

ORGANIZATIONAL DYNAMICS AS DRIVERS OF STRUCTURE

In creating links and bringing them into play, functional and project managers become essential to the flow of knowledge, inventions, and progress, as they establish a network that creates a dynamic between goals and needs and timelines on one side and skills and passions and drives on the other. When needs do not match passion, the flow of projects can be slowed down to a halt, even with opportunities that promise major breakthroughs. Recall the complexity of moving the project that appeared to be a result of a clash of titans with strong personalities but was actually a mismatch in organizational goals. It is out of this rich, necessary network with its ongoing toggle between two organizations that innovation flows. To be meaningful, links must be strong enough to resist the push and pull that comes with the high stakes of delivering technology. But to be successful it is not sufficient to be just well connected. What is needed is connections based on trust and shared values and, even better, friendship. Meaningful connections fire the spirit that opens dialogue, attracts resources, finds solutions, stretches minds, and persuades supporters, key to understanding opportunities, connecting dots, and creating engagement. Even though the pressure of a high-priority, high-visibility project may persuade us to just move, the time invested in developing and leaning on rich relationships to deliver on your responsibility never ceases to pay off.

As counterpoint, Kirsten Steinmeier brings to life the impact of not doing so as she relates, "I was recently asked to help with 3-D forming of glass, pressing or vacuum forming of these funny-shaped things, and I was never invited to a project meeting. I was asked a question by e-mail—that is a usual start—but it was just, 'Please answer this question.' They think that they have the question that they need answered, but I was pretty sure that they did not have that right yet. I was never engaged, I had no idea who the leader was, who was making decisions, what was important, so I had many other things to work on and it was easy to pass on this one."

But one could argue further, as Andrew Hargadon does in his "Nexus Workers" concept, that innovation is about connecting, not inventing, through social relationships and technological connections. For breakthroughs to come to life, you need to start with a group that brings together both a sense of freedom and a clear organization: a clearly defined culture that allows the intuition—the sense of possibility—to emerge, and a clear structure—with attitudes and behaviors clearly spelled out—that provides practitioners with an ability to describe their own role. Internally, this allows easy workflow *within* the group. The next ingredient, the essential one in connecting to the external groups needed to make an idea happen, is a sense of empowerment to take these attitudes and behaviors beyond, to the larger organization. It is from here that innovation emerges, from the ability to navigate and influence the external organization. It goes beyond connecting; it takes the enabling of individuals, the helping to make sense of opportunities, the creating and combining of resources, to advance a program or a cause.

Every project is a universe with different initial parameters and needs as well as different levels of complexity. Three efforts of the creation of networks to deliver innovation, with varying degrees of complexity, bring to life the process of understanding a challenge and creating the network—from an internal group to a larger organization—to deliver the breakthrough.

What Does the World Need?
Define Roles Clearly to Deliver Results

In the late 1990s we had an experience of big consequences that brings this point to life. This first case starts with two clearly defined positions: the need of the display business unit to deliver a new glass to the marketplace and the responsibility of the glass research group in defining the composition for such glass. The rules of the game, however, were initially eluding us.

After entering the display market with the solid position of relying on a unique and proprietary manufacturing process that produced the world's highest-quality precision glass, the display business was in need of a new glass composition, one that would allow Corning to distance itself from the competition. I was responsible for glass research and so had responsibility for delivering the future for this business unit. On the receiving end, the development leader was Jim Brosner, a bright scientist with a Ph.D. from Cornell who would later rise to have responsibility for all flat-glass technology development for the business and whom I had met on my very first day at Corning. I had learned as much from Jim about experimental techniques in chemical vapor deposition as I had about running and weight training—activities we both enjoyed for years to come—and we also shared time flying kites and doing other parenting duties and developing a strong and trusting friendship.

In his search for glasses that offered a differential advantage, Jim, who had previously done research in glass himself, relied on his long-term relationship with our researchers, and the process of identification of desirable glass properties marched along informal ties for some time. Jim, guided by his marketing manager Jonathan Bowen, who had a good understanding of the market from his dependable customer connections, would define property requirements as goals for glass composition. Our scientists would respond with samples and the glass would be taken for the reaction of customers. We were all comfortable with this process, and in terms of delivering on requirements there was no concern. The issue came as customers reacted to new glass proposals and the complexity of the market grew; what was good for one would be of little interest to the next.

After several of these attempts it became clear that there was a need to add a level of sophistication to our definition of roles and links and responsibilities. My leadership role in glass research made it my responsibility to demand definition of clear glass property targets that were based on a thorough understanding of the market as a whole. In his role in marketing, Jim was responsible for translating his understanding into specific requirements.

In a meeting that lasted well into the evening, I was clear with Jim and Jonathan that we would halt all efforts aimed at developing new glass compositions for display unless we had a clear definition, based on market research, of properties that would deliver a strong enough differential advantage to receive wide market endorsement and gain purchase orders. Jointly, we created a list of glass attributes that could be tailored and the advantages they would bring to customer processing or product performance.

It took six months of well-designed market research, most of which the Jim-and-Jon team carried out in countries on the eastern rim of the Pacific Ocean, aided by Jon's solid connections into customers' minds and Jim's understanding and rigor in mining them. Six months during which, other than that driven by scientific intuition and curiosity, there were no investigations done by the glass research group on projects for display glass. At the end of this period, Jim and Jon came back with a clear definition of what a winning glass—one whose physical properties would bring maximum competitive impact to the majority of customers, rather than one tailored specifically for one or two of them—would look like. This enabled the creation of a project with clear goals: a glass composition offering greater dimensional stability with temperature variation and *simultaneously* lowering weight without losing, of course, the viscosity requirements demanded by Corning's proprietary forming process. With Isabel Lopez doing composition work, the glass research group developed a composition that not only delivered the desired properties but did so smoothly enough to go from research directly into production without requiring the glass compositional adjustments that typify intervening plant trials. In becoming the standard by which other glasses in the market would be measured, this glass paved the way to Corning's lasting technological supremacy in display glasses.

Reflecting after years had gone by on the impact to the business, Jim Brosner would say, "This glass was an important factor in the sustained success of the LCD platform itself. At that time, LCDs were largely landlocked in the notebook and desktop monitor application, and the industry then could be characterized by a languid pace of innovation. Corning's new glass was a component in the great breakout of the LCD technology to win in TV and to be omnipresent in a great diversity of smaller applications."

While at times the role of research is to press for clear definition of attributes and an immediate focus on the present, at other times the sight needs to be focused on the future, in pursuit of a dream that not even fellow researchers can visualize. And then research leaders have to become steadfast defenders of the need for the open space and open time that impassioned practitioners crave. For at times they not only can visualize what for others are just dreams, they can even envision how to make it to the final goal. Early stages call for vision, but they also call for sense. The sense that guides a dream, aligns with strategy, and creates partnerships that deliver.

In Search of the Holy Grail
Defend and Align the Space of Dreams

The odds against success in this second case were so great that it was hard to predict success, and had it not been for a talented project leader it might not have happened. The glass research group had a clear vision of the potential and a highly competitive multi-option approach, both for composition and for process. It needed a major, complex project to sort these out. But another significant challenge would be to overcome the skepticism of the commercial team—based on their estimated 5 percent probability of success—and turn them from nonbelievers to endorsers, and ultimately to supporters.

He had been an unusual recruit for glass research, an organization used to hiring scientists that have the potential to become glass researchers and then training them, as the vast majority of universities do not offer degrees in glass science at the level at which Corning operates. Unlike most new hires, who go through a learning curve and become productive after their first year, Rabbindrana Raja arrived with a sophisticated understanding of glass structure and properties and was comfortable with state-of-the-art techniques. So we should not have been surprised with his unusual start. After a warm-up period on a project of his own choosing, he was ready to hit the ball out of the park with a bold new proposal.

It was early in the first decade of the twenty-first century and the Corning technology group was going through a period when direction for the research group was entrusted to a triumvirate of directors. Reporting to these were the people responsible for the functional management of the core competencies, a group of nineteen directors in all. The culture was in a period of transition and group dynamics were made difficult by the lack of internal agreement among the nineteen on corporate strategic direction and, in turn, on the strategic direction of research. In an effort to encourage participation and transparency for the process of defining the research project portfolio, the triumvirate had asked all nineteen core technology directors to make presentations to the entire group outlining the merits of projects coming from our groups.

Included in my portfolio was Rabbindrana's proposal for an exploratory research project to deliver what amounted to the decades-long holy grail of single-mode optical fiber manufacturers: a fiber that would lower transmission losses by 25 percent from the level that had been established thirty years prior. At the time, the attainable level of transmission losses had been deeply entrenched in the industry and even a 10 percent reduction was considered a worthy goal. Much effort, time, and resources had been invested on this pursuit by the best scientists at the world's premier industrial research labs, but there was little progress to show. There was only one Japanese manufacturer offering losses below the industry standard, and it was well known that in order to do so, fiber draw speeds needed to be slowed down to 5 percent of standard practice. In Rabbindrana's mind, though, it was a simple matter of understanding how chemistry affects the fundamental physics of the glass system. To the collection of optical physicists and systems engineers with years in the field of telecommunications, fibers, and devices, the proposal was another "pie in the sky," "not worthy of our time" project and, as such, not worthy of inclusion in the research portfolio.

Both Rabbindrana and I knew intuitively that he was on to something. It was easy to understand; the rationale was solid and the scientific predictions followed. We pressed on with the oldest trick known to research managers: creating space for an exploratory project that does not appear in the portfolio. Rabbindrana's idea was simple: move away from the single-component system of today's fibers—pure silica—and, through the addition of the right level of a potassium "contaminant," soften the glass just enough to lower scattering losses yet not too much to introduce damaging impurities. As the project grew from a one-person effort to the larger resources required for a demonstration of principle, the need for official project definition and a project manager became apparent.

Looking ahead at the complexity this project was likely to encounter during its evolution, we needed to find a project manager with the skills to address numerous complex scientific problems; to rationalize them and prioritize a series of theoretical, modeling, and underlying experimental needs; and to structure team activities in sequence to arrive at a solution. An additional requirement would likely be—in the event of strong commercial pull—an ability to do all of the above within tight timelines. Ideally, should the project result in a technology transfer into manufacturing, there was the additional requirement for the candidate to have strong connections to Corning's fiber manufacturing community.

We did not have to look far. In our own glass research group we had Isabel Lopez, a person who, though new to project management, met all the job requirements and had repeatedly accomplished the translation of fundamental understandings into process improvements for Corning's fiber plant facility in the United States. This would be a stretching experience for Isabel, one that would enable her to add project management to her already demonstrated skills as technical and functional leader. She moved into the project judiciously, though not effortlessly. As understanding drove results, the project gained credibility and support, first from the development group and then from the plant—the support from the commercial unit would have to wait.

As the project gained in support downstream, another social process was taking place upstream within research, with success inviting competition. Ideas and approaches that, though disruptive to the project itself, could not be ignored were coming into the project from both inside and out. With her ability to encompass a wide spectrum of ideas, prioritize them, and define team activities to arrive at a solution, Isabel would go to task over and over again. Two approaches led in the final turn. The first was Rabbindrana's approach for potassium doping, which though feasible was technically the most challenging to implement at the plant. It had reproducibly demonstrated an impressive 30 percent reduction in transmission loss for fiber drawn at the development facility. The second compositional approach was introducing a lower level of the same dopant, which enabled a simpler implementation at the plant but had a demonstrated reduction in loss of only 12 percent. In light of technical difficulty and delivery time, Rabbindrana's was deemed long term relative to the shorter term of the competing approach.

Team dynamics offered all the challenges that project and functional managers together can handle. In those roles, Isabel and I would confer often in addressing the needs of the strong passions—and stronger behavior—of the most ardent proponents of each approach, some of whom could get irritated at each other for even minor things, and also of the doubters and the volunteers who descended in search of free glory, or who saw themselves as free facilitators.

With the intention of delivering two succeeding generations of low-loss fiber, the second approach went to manufacturing and achieved transmission quality unsurpassed in the market while being manufactured at regular manufacturing fiber draw speeds, a double trophy in a game of champions. But in time not all intentions materialized. The market changed and the efforts to take the ultra-low-loss fiber promised *and* delivered by Rabbindrana's approach from development to the manufacturing plant never saw the light of the market. It was the right thing for the business, but the loss, perhaps, befell the world.

Our role as leaders is to have the vision to understand what the organization needs and the wherewithal to put it together and make it happen, to create and defend an *impassioned* organization that combines elements of hierarchy with elements of anarchy: strategy, direction, and leadership from the top; ideas and invention from below, side-to-side, across, and over the top; coordinated delivery and execution. In addition to a role as receiver of requests from the commercial and manufacturing units, core competency leaders have an important role in anticipating opportunities for future growth. Because growth opportunities are not pressing issues in the here-and-now, the role of creating and propelling them is difficult, often unwelcome, and highly demanding. Making things more complicated is that the farther out the opportunity, the lower the sense of urgency and the greater the complexity and uncertainty. This is when clear definition of roles and links is of utmost importance. It requires an organization that is clearly defined and flexible, players that are comfortable in their roles and courageous enough to stretch them, links that are based on trust and resiliency. But then it may deliver the unexpected.

A Filter for Europe
A Strong Partnership of Skills and Trust Pays Off

The complexity of this third case is enhanced by the expected disparity of strategic focus between research and commercial groups mentioned previously. In this case there was a clear definition of market need shared by both groups and a clear plan for the research group that called for a race with many candidates. The challenge was to gain the strategic support of the commercial team to make the innovation happen.

It would prove to be one of the most complex, fast-moving, and challenging of programs with the least initial business support that anybody would think of starting. But the view from research, the view that places on the shoulders of the research organization the responsibility to create opportunities for growth, demanded that it be set in motion. And a strong tie between the research and development leaders made it happen.

Along the path from research to the business unit the first stop is, of course, development. Running the development group and in the role of first receiver from research was Peter Blanchard, a red-bearded French scientist with whom I enjoyed exchanging Tour de France results as much as learning about the chateaus of the Loire valley. As counterparts in the technology delivery process we had maintained healthy ties with frequent meetings, and all during the diesel threat saga he had shared the perspective of research and supported the need for exploration of new approaches.

After establishing itself nearly thirty years earlier as a leading force in automotive emissions control following the invention of a novel proprietary process for the extrusion of an equally proprietary material into honeycomb substrates, Corning's environmental products business was facing a serious threat. In the beginning of the twenty-first century, market growth for diesel-powered passenger cars in Europe offered a nice opportunity for expansion of the existing diesel product line from heavy-duty applications to light-duty applications, new to Corning. Original attempts at addressing both auto and diesel market segments with the same product were running into serious performance challenges. At the same time, the market was seeing the introduction of a competing new material that could withstand the harsh diesel environment. The drawbacks were cracking concerns stemming from its design: gluing segments to form a cylinder in an orange-like geometry to make up for the shortcomings of their material.

The business was taking the threat seriously and had responded accordingly, running applied research projects in its development organization with three different approaches, one for each of the current, the competing, and a totally new material. Progress was being made, but it was hard to call the race, as many technical hurdles remained unsolved. As the person responsible for creating opportunities through new materials, and fully aware of this responsibility and of the unlocked potential of the world of materials, I would ask questions and probe and encourage and prod the scientists in inorganic technologies—in the creativity room, at lunch, in the hallways—until they were all in search of materials that could *intrinsically* survive diesel conditions *and* that we had a chance of making by a reasonable manufacturing process.

The search ignited imaginations and soon we had an expanding number of candidates, a good starting position for a research project. In the development group, Peter Blanchard stood alone in understanding that it was imperative to respond to the threat with a no-holds-barred effort in search for new materials. But the business unit, with pressing issues for its commercial group and all hands in its development group full, was not considering this new potential project. In fact, they were uncertain that there would be room for a new material in the marketplace.

My responsibility as leader of research, though, required me to press ahead, and so I initiated a series of small exploratory efforts in search of new materials. And I was lucky— indeed, the business was lucky, though they did not know it then—to have in Peter an ally in development, an honest ally who believed in the cause as much as we in research did. Early results were promising, and, as with the informal and independent efforts that typify exploratory research, they were being loosely observed rather than formally coordinated. We were growing from two to four and, soon after, to six different potential materials that could be serious contenders. Others had already been cast aside.

Thinking about the skills needed by a project manager to succeed in this mission was dizzying. We would need somebody who could lead a multipronged technical team and could open discussions on different approaches, who would bring to the table several different viewpoints and guide them to effective collaboration. Somebody who could aptly manage the ensuing—and necessary—conflict, and if successful who could take the team from being the dark horse with six or eight parallel approaches—all of them behind the division's own approaches—to being the lead approach and delivering the one successful candidate. And, just to make it simpler, it would be ideal if we could find somebody who understood business strategy but also the need to deliver sound, technology-based solutions.

I searched my head and heart, consulted with different organizations, and interviewed candidates. I finally thought of Jeff Major, whom I knew both as an exploratory researcher from the first group I joined at Corning—where we got to know each other as we adapted to rural Corning and its surroundings while responding to the challenges of parenthood—and as a project manager from my days in consumer products. In addition to his commercial/technology dual experience, he had technical competence in a variety of fields, from organic to inorganic chemistry, from enzymes to catalysis. Our careers had evolved along different paths and he was not part of any of my groups. At that point, though, working in the critical area of bottom-of-draw protective coatings for display glasses, I knew that he was "eager for a new challenge. A new, tough challenge," he told me. I knew I had found our project manager.

Finding the right person to lead the project was but the first step. Even if we were successful at identifying a new material and could prove that it could be manufactured and that it had all the required properties, it would languish in the research labs if it did not find its place in the strategic plan of the business unit. Fortunately, the first requirement—a solid research-development alliance—had already been met. With a solid relationship with Peter and with a shared common vision, we plotted to saddle Jeff not just with the responsibility of a regular project manager, but with a double reporting relationship. He would indeed run a research project, but, we reasoned, it was important for the commercial organization to feel a sense of ownership for the project expressed by a reporting tie, one that we hoped would translate into support and eventually a transfer into manufacturing. So, in a gamble that defied established roles, Peter took the *functional* responsibility for the project while I kept the *project* responsibility. This made it a *research* project run *by* development *for* research, rather than the other, more traditional, way around. It was an unorthodox organization structure, but it was a key to success.

And from the business perspective, this made all the difference. A decade later, Peter would reflect on this key, though unconventional, reporting structure: "A key driver of the organizational structure we decided to put in place was Jeff Major. At the time there were several technology approaches considered in research. They were spread over several groups ranging from glass research, ceramic research, and even surface research. Given the silo-sensitive research dynamics, it was very important for me to find someone and an organizational structure that would prevent the research project manager from being accused of bias for one group versus another when making decisions. In this respect, having Jeff functionally reporting to the development directorate provided an additional enabler of his ability to operate effectively."

After months of exploration and progress, of experimentation, down selection, and even late introduction of new candidates under the rigor and rational decision making that Jeff imposed on the team, Peter and I shared the feeling that it was time to gain the support of the business leaders.

Frank Spencer was the respected general manager for the business unit. He was a strategy-focused leader with the panache, seldom found in corporate settings but commonly seen in theater majors like himself, to enthrall audiences. We knew him well and had learned to trust him, and we knew he was open to new ideas and responded to articulate argumentation.

As is often the case with general managers, his time was short and he could only meet with our team after hours, but this made no difference to the people working on the project. Project manager and team—no longer the collection of separate efforts of earlier days—had reached a sophisticated level of understanding of external market dynamics and the unfolding of the business strategy within the existing diesel product platform, and of technical requirements and timelines to match their mastery of ceramics, processing, and testing. They went all out to fight for the lifeline of the project: the support of the business unit.

After their presentation, Frank saw the value of the approach and responded by providing support for our effort in the search for new materials that would give Corning a competitive advantage in the diesel passenger car segments. In closing the meeting, he agreed to add this project to the official business-sponsored portfolio following our down selection to the candidates that met a given minimum of property requirements. We knew we could count on Frank's word, and we did.

The result would have been hard to predict a couple of years earlier. By taking a project from early research on a fast track all the way down to manufacturing, the project leader and team delivered a new material that created new strategic space for the business, emerging as a viable solution to the needs of diesel light-duty vehicles and enjoying early acceptance by lead customers who recognized its superior performance and liked its lower cost. The business unit was positioned to use it as their opening to the European diesel passenger car market.

After some years Frank Spencer, reflecting on the impact of the project on the business and with the perspective afforded by the passage of time, would summarize: "Not only did the feat delivered by this team—commercialization of a new filter in ten months, based on a completely new material—allow us to become the largest supplier of diesel filters to the European diesel car leader, but it took our relationship with this customer to a whole new level. They recognized our 'technology competence' and our demonstrated ability to take risks, exercise judgment, and deliver large-scale innovation. And they, in turn, gave us an unprecedented degree of flexibility in our business relationship and developed a reliance on what we can do when challenged by difficult problems, and as a result our business together grew rapidly. The relationship was taken to a whole new level from there on. They referred to our team that delivered this new technology as 'the dream team.' And the dream team it indeed was."

To excel at breakthrough innovation you must first create a culture, provide it with a clear structure, and exhibit the behaviors that support the culture and the structure of the organization. This is not necessarily easy. It may be easier at times to exhibit behaviors supportive of culture—values that are clearly defined provide efficient guardrails to keep all in—than to define actions in conformance with roles. But the understanding of role in guiding actions is of particular importance for the leader. It is not about curtailing initiative, but about understanding where the role of other players start and yours ends. Taking over the responsibilities of others in the zeal of making a project move on a fast track seldom helps it along. At best, it brings confusion and demotivation, the very forces that you need to avoid in project delivery, particularly in fast, complex project delivery.

Every group has experienced high-visibility, high-urgency projects that are organizational "musts" and that, in commanding top priority from all levels, create a frenzy of activity that makes people forget their roles. Though it is tempting at times to believe otherwise, it is not the role of managers, directors, or vice presidents to make technical decisions, or to overpower project meetings by their sheer numbers, or to harass testing technicians in a daily pursuit of data for them to quote. The principle is simple: the greater the adherence to the roles *for all levels* of the organization, the easier the coordination of delivery and execution.

MY PERSONAL JOURNEY

On My Way to France

COMING BACK FROM THE TWO-HOUR DRIVE from Rochester after my annual mammogram and still feeling the pain of the needle biopsy that to my good fortune turned out benign—only a five-year reprieve as luck would have it—I attended the patent award dinner, a major corporate event at Corning, during which Rob Stanley, Corning's CTO, approached me with a simple question: "Would you be interested in an international assignment?" Without hesitation my answer was a resounding "Absolutely!" He stopped short of a discussion and moved on to the next person.

Rob was an experienced technology officer who danced on the floor of corporate executives and boards of directors with ease and who had the strong support of upper leadership for the technology community to show as a result. A man with a heart and an interest in people, the past couple of years under his direction had been a time when results flowed and spirits were high. Our group reflected that, both in performance and in spirit. But for me those two years had tested my fortitude and ability to stay centered.

Along my career, I had enjoyed a balance of expansivity

and guidance afforded by my supervisors. I had learned from them and had been given the space to liberate my values and develop my own style. But my current experience had been a sharp departure from that path. For reasons that were—and to this day remain—paradoxical to all, in the previous two years my expectations ran into a hard wall, and in that assignment the atmosphere was inconsistent with the reality I had previously experienced: where I had found trust I now met lack of support; where I was used to constructive debate I now encountered resistance to new perspectives; where I was used to reliance there was an absence of opportunities. My doors— to participation, to opportunities—and my voice were being shut in a way that was as apparent as it was puzzling to all those witnessing it: my peers, my groups, senior leadership. This is a situation most people will find at one point in their careers, even though the struggle feels unique and personal.

In an effort to continue to rely on two leaders who were at an impasse, top management went to *one* of them for clues that would solve the riddle and find an end to the situation: they came to me for answers and solutions. I was clear in sharing my experience in conflict management that it takes *two* willing people to move the needle, not just one. Nevertheless, I was willing to do my part. But despite my sincere efforts at building an alliance and addressing the situation directly with my supervisor, he would not engage and no one could find answers. I was headed for a train wreck, and had it not been for the support and recognition—even protection—that the continued high performance of my groups gained me, my derailing would have been unavoidable.

In his search for answers to the conundrum, Rob Stanley found a clever solution to two situations that he faced at the time: a decision on redefining or ending Corning's research lab in France, and the space and support I so dearly needed. By bringing me into his staff and sending me overseas to define the future of the technology center, he solved both. Though I would have preferred to see senior leadership embrace conflict and address the core of the issue, I knew the territory and what to expect. Taking it for what it was, a pat on the back and an endorsement, I walked toward my new assignment. A new life experience awaited me.

Provide Authentic Leadership

THE ROLE OF LEADING CREATIVE TEAMS—inspiring seasoned practitioners to follow the spark of an idea wherever it may lead and facilitating the delivery of results that are new to the world— covers a wide spectrum of responsibilities, from providing strategy and direction to being responsible for coordinating delivery and execution, to the creation and sheltering of a culture. In addition to these large-scale strategy-setting and decision-making functions, impassioned teams need leaders who make things happen in the day-to-day life of a project, in a way that touches lives and further creates culture. The necessary dimensions are many: a broad perspective based on connection to all players, both inside and outside the team; the cross-fertilization of ideas and creation of networks that bring different streams together; going to bat for resources; recognition of accomplishments and promotion of results and career advancement; creation of demands and raising the bar; providing an example of "walking the path"; and listening, listening, listening.

Needless to say, leading fast-paced innovation teams puts the most seasoned of leaders to the test. To hold together the responsibilities of the role, a successful leader needs backbone, moral fiber, chutzpah, and spiritual fortitude. But it does not stop there. To guide intense, high-energy teams, a leader needs to be passionate; impassioned practitioners are naturally at odds with apathetic leadership and the ambiguous results it elicits. But a leader's passion must be authentic; it cannot be put on or imposed from outside. Leaders need to be true to themselves while carrying out their roles. Following a recipe and going through the mechanics, even if the symbols are there, will neither create a culture nor motivate teams.

Ultimately, for leaders to be able to successfully maintain the peak performance that the role demands, they need to run both hot and cold at the same time: impassioned and detached. The passionate, energizing aspect is key to the motivational and inspirational facet of the leader. But it is detachment that enables the leader to guide the raft through whitewater. Detachment arises from awareness of what is *really* happening, from the understanding that your participation is required, but your control is not. A detached leader can afford to put her energy into nurturing, not controlling.

The complexity of the role of leader and the intensity of the demands on the self raise the question of what principles leaders need to rely on for support in staying centered, principles that allow them to go beyond simply maintaining their sanity to experiencing their role as a vehicle for individual freedom and an opportunity to express their own fulfillment.

In my own experience the answer to this question started with our guru Dasa—admittedly an unlikely character in the corporate arena—who prompted my search on how to live out the realization of my true nature in my daily work. Getting to know him after taking his constructive feedback workshop early in my managerial career initiated a lifelong learning that would take me from learning how to provide transformative feedback to guidance on being an authentic leader. Dasa had the wisdom and ability to be supportive and relentless at the same time, and with him I explored the concepts of spirit of leadership, empowerment and interdependence, service and support, self-awareness and acceptance, and *Wisdom at Work*—to quote the title of one of his books. The exploration opened the door to many rich concepts, and the practice of going deeper into consciousness soon proved to demand commitment, honesty, and high doses of courage. But in time I also came to learn about the balance and detachment that the practice enables, one on which you learn to rely when facing the toughest of situations. My experience in France was about to provide me with a beautiful occasion to put it all together in a new context.

Leading for Change
Respond to the Challenge

The offer to run Corning's lab in France was one that I accepted with gusto. Earlier in our careers, my husband and I had lived in Germany for three years while working at the Max Planck Institüt for Geochemistry, an experience we had greatly enjoyed, and I looked forward to being back in Europe. Throughout the years I had gotten to know many of the scientists at the Fontainebleau Research Center—a name given to the research lab by its flamboyant director in an effort to reflect the prestige of this well-known location—through visits to the lab and through collaborations. I was happy at the prospect of leading a self-standing part of Corning's large international technology community, and I was comfortable with the assignment. The multidimensionality of the role that I was stepping into as an agent of change and organizational redefinition would pose a demanding, fascinating, and absorbing challenge.

Corning had just gotten past what its own leaders defined as a "near-death experience," the post-photonics bubble period of soul searching and organizational renewal that brought the company back to life. During the search for survival, the technology community had to slash a series of laboratories throughout the world that had been acquired during the previous years. The decision regarding the Fontainebleau Research Center, which had been part of the technology community for decades, was particularly heart-wrenching. It came down to the wire and in the end the choice was to keep it but to redefine its role within the technology community *and* relative to the business units. At about one-tenth the size of Corning's flagship research and development facility in upstate New York, the French laboratory had for years emulated it, finding itself in an ill-defined younger-sibling position. The French lab had first-rate scientific and engineering personnel with a broad array of backgrounds addressing research and development projects in an equally wide number of fields, but it lacked a clear definition of its strategic value. In the words of the outgoing CEO, what the corporate leadership wanted was for "the role of the French lab to be so clearly defined that nobody in the corporation will ask themselves the question 'Why do we have a lab in France?'"

In my mind, my success in the role had to start with the language. Though in multinational corporations leadership often gets by in the corporate mother tongue, I felt strongly that in order to lead a community one needs to be accepted as part of them. Not to pretend to be one of them, but to be able to integrate with them and share their world—and read the news, watch major events, interact with community leaders, and negotiate with union leaders. My high school French had not been dusted off for decades, and part of it had been forgotten in my attempts to learn German many years before, but I was able to recover it during a two-week immersion course in Rochester—the third week would have to wait until after my installation in France.

The lab received well that initial address in French during my first communications meeting with them, but it was my opening a Q&A session, also in French, that made them feel that I was for real, that in answering their questions they could be sure I was not relying on memorized text. My message to them was clear: the priority of defining the role of the lab had a key theme, and that theme was alignment. We could not just be a superior French center, we needed to prove ourselves by bringing value to the corporate business and technology directions. If we defined ourselves in a role that was *key* to the major divisions and *unique* within the technology group, and if we delivered outstanding performances that made us vital to business operations, the existence of a lab in Europe would become a business imperative. In understanding the importance of positioning the lab not just as a French entity, but as a European center, I started talking about the European lab, rather than the French lab, and so from that first meeting I introduced the vision of becoming a port of access to European science and technology. And, lastly, for the lab's own vibrancy, we needed to maintain a rich effort in exploratory research. Those four areas—a key role for the business, unique competencies within research, port of access to Europe, and rich exploration—were central to my vision and became the defining actions for our joint mission. Thus started three years of high intensity, high engagement on the part of all that transformed the lab in role, strategic direction, makeup, and culture. Three years that challenged as much as they enriched the lives of all of us as we all gave our best.

I inherited a group of hard-working, bright managers, each of whom was responsible for a group of people, for some research, in some cases development activities, and in others specific projects. They knew their people, who in turn respected them well, were well versed in the technologies under them, and were accustomed to following the director. I came out of our first meetings puzzled about the organization, whereas my managers came out frustrated by my constant drilling about roles, links, and responsibilities and resistant to my approach of empowerment and interdependence. They were more comfortable with the previous system of hierarchical authority, and I was more interested in getting to know the person that lay behind each of the managers.

My cultural learning was under way when I came to understand two theses central to my new surroundings: the insistence on maintaining a clear delineation between work and personal life, and the importance of the number of subordinates as a marker of professional advancement. The former imprinted the nature of the exchanges between supervisor and employees within and outside the laboratory; the latter defined the structural organization of the workplace. To create a culture of empowerment where people can be ahead of the facts, one that encourages every person to follow their spark against all obstacles and supports them in so doing, it was important to sway some of these cultural tendencies without losing the richness of the existing culture.

Getting to know my direct reports, making them comfortable enough to open up and share their interests and activities, making them aware of their driving forces as well as their conditioned responses, were priorities. Creating an organizational structure that supported our vision and mission and that was embraced by my staff and by the lab as a whole was another one. But, though alone in a new country, I would not go so far as attempting to buckle their cultural resistance to socializing with the boss outside of work.

We set to work creating a cohesive leadership team, sharing a vision and making it happen. More than anything, I wanted a group of empowered people who could bring out their best in thought and action, with whom I could have a dynamic give and take, and who would stand up to my views and challenge them and in so doing make the total be more than the sum of its parts. I wanted them to take charge of their high performance as much as of their happiness and to share with me the revitalization of the organization so we could shape it in harmony with our shared values. And I wanted them to understand that while we were sharing the power of leadership in creating a meaningful organization together, I remained accountable for its success.

Our staff meetings started having a strong strategic component in addition to the managerial aspects needed to do things right, with which they had significant experience. After several months, in an effort to inject more power to our team-building efforts, I called in Dasa and Rob McLaughlin, the U.S.–based director of human resources for the international corporate technology community, to help me lead two- and three-day semiannual leadership retreats.

I wanted these occasions to be more than special opportunities for learning about strategy and leadership, empowerment and courage, integrity and self-awareness. I also wanted them to be opportunities to strengthen the ties that bind, to learn to trust and rely on each other, and simply to have fun and feel special. And so I gave Nathalie Gordon—a six-foot-tall French woman with surprisingly perfect New Zealand–accented English acquired as a young bride in that country and who as my administrative assistant became my most exacting daily French instructor—full range for her creativity in finding us locations conducive to inspiring our spirit and indulging our style. She did not disappoint any of us as she discovered and negotiated with lodges in small French villages, in chateaus in the campagne Française, or in restaurants and inns in wine country. The meals were succulent and the lodgings comfortable, but the richness came from the demanding sessions, where concepts were challenged, attitudes were questioned, and being true to self was expected. The level of comfort with creative conflict was raised, recruiting practices reviewed, values discussed and listed, the nature of the organization argued, and self-awareness fully explored.

We relied on outdoor activities such as rope courses and rock climbing as well as indoor activities such as guitar playing and singing to teach the group to trust each other and to simply play and have fun. We did things culturally backwards—cheese with crackers as appetizer rather than third course, our own French classical guitarist playing American blues—to explore other cultures, but most importantly to explore ourselves. A culture was being created, a future was being envisioned, and the stage was being set for the amazing to occur.

Attitudes that the lab was exceptional by virtue of its being French changed to a view of a lab whose richness stems from reaching out to the larger Europe. The practice of relying on headhunters as the main recruiting tool was replaced by hiring through personal connections and referrals. After an initial period of having to demand non-French candidates for every opening, the lab got a facelift as scientists from countries ranging from Germany, England, and Italy, to Romania, India, and Madagascar joined its ranks. The culture was changing, the bar was being raised, the boundaries lifted.

The definition of the role of the lab as being key to the business units was central to the repositioning of the center within the corporation. Though Corning is an active player in European technology markets, the lab had not established itself with a specific role in support of the business units with activities in that continent. By virtue of its location, being defined as essential to the business operations in Europe was a must. Prior to moving to France, I had discussions with three general managers and we had jointly identified the intersection between their pressing technology and customer needs and our skills and assets: the lab would support the immediate customer needs of the diesel passenger car market for Corning's environmental technologies business, support the emerging high-throughput screening technology needs of the life sciences business, and push the state-of-the-art of precision hot glass forming for the display business. Several months later, funding for new installations and equipment had been approved. The redefinition now rested on the creation of a clear organizational structure to support and deliver the mission.

Though it would have been simple to create a new structure by dictum, it was important that my staff, the leadership of the lab, gather their minds and hearts around the imperative, as they, in turn, would be passing the word and the spirit along to their people. Long and rigorous discussions around roles, links, and responsibilities, the difference in roles and skills required of functional and project managers, and the thorny issue of the meaning of leadership in the absence of direct reports led us there. The final product, a well-defined structure that had been clear to me early in my engagement, one that made it unambiguous who was to deliver technology for the business, who ran projects, and who was responsible for creating and maintaining core competencies, was endorsed and embraced by the whole leadership team. And most importantly, each member of the staff understood his role, understood the skills he brought to the role, and could begin to see work as a means to the realization of his potential. The process of engaging the business units, of creating strong personal links and responding to their business needs, of anticipating technology demands and establishing capabilities, had taken its first steps.

A second central repositioning theme was the ability to unequivocally define the function of the lab within Corning's research community, and so it was important to restrict activities and eliminate duplication—always harder than expanding. The creativity of the researchers had enabled the lab to develop expertise in many subjects and pursue projects in divergent directions. The need was not one of harnessing creativity, but of directing it to specific areas unique within corporate research while fostering a culture where innovation thrives and, by doing so, becoming the undisputed center of excellence for a short list of competencies for the corporation. There were already several such areas, in glass forming, in organic materials, and in high-temperature glass-ceramic forming and processing, though they were not unique. Negotiations this time needed to be with the leadership of Corning's central lab, so I engaged in long and eventually productive discussions with my colleagues on the other side of the Atlantic, redefining efforts and responsibilities and ultimately benefiting all sides. Our identity was emerging as distinct, valuable, and essential.

The overall population at the center felt the progress by the way their groups shifted focus, responsibilities, and reporting structure, but also by the new breath of openness that they felt in the air. My open-door policy was broadly accepted and the initial trickle of visitors with hesitation in their voices grew to a larger stream of scientists and technicians full of ideas, concerns, opportunities, and life situations. Ideas and requests for new equipment, for support of union-sanctioned activities, for the summer or Christmas parties, for a larger budget for a project, for advice on cultural integration, for a creativity room of their own, were just part of the mélange. At the café at lunchtime, I was learning about French politicians and labor union leaders while sharing my passion for the Tour de France with the technicians, and after hours I was being humbled by them in my attempts to play squash.

Negotiations with the unions, which had started with the traditional tension, were being met with honesty, transparency, and even humor, and they moved from a confrontation of opposite sides to a representation of different sides working for not just a surviving, but a thriving organization. In the office, I continued to improve my French by writing personal birthday cards to each employee in Nathalie-sanctioned grammar. In their dealings with their managers, employees were being consulted, prodded, challenged, supported. The creativity room and the café for larger crowds became the center of celebrations for project milestones or parties for the birthdays of the month. Together we were building a culture of excitement and commitment to performance where everybody wanted to do their part. And the results were being validated by the frequent visitors from inside and outside business and technology groups alike, interested in our results and exchanges and happy to enjoy delightful French meals in the surrounding towns. The center and its leadership started playing a more visible and influential role in the community, meeting with local government representatives, attending museum functions, and making donations to civic societies. The lab was becoming a hub and a force, and the energy was palpable.

More than two years into the process the lab continued to be known as the Fontainebleau Research Center, a name that no longer reflected its mission or scope. Once again, it was important that the understanding of this identity evolution came from within rather than by mandate so that, just as the work that was being done jointly with everybody's best effort, a new name could be embraced by all and become a source of motivation. And so it did, during one of our semiannual leadership retreats, as a response to a dare to the team with the best succinct definition of the lab as it stood then, with a case of French wine as a prize for the best description. The exercise was about understanding role, mission, and vision, and we dug deep to mine it and to go beyond. After arguing about merits, generalities, and specifics, the leadership team clearly felt that the lab was now about technology in the broad sense and that the arena had gone beyond the country and was now Europe.

They went on to vote for Corning European Technology Center as the best descriptor and suggested themselves to propose this as a name change to the CTO. And so it came to be, to the amazement of CTO Rob Stanley, who "expected great things but never in a million years dreamed of being able to change the name." As to the desire of the outgoing CEO that people no longer have a reason for asking "Why a lab in Europe?" He got it fulfilled, with top leadership agreeing: "The Management Committee appreciates and values the lab at this time. That was not the case before she got there," and, "The lab used to be very starry-eyed and wanted to be independent, running its own agenda, searching for the next big thing. It's much more integrated with the corporate initiatives and with corporate technical strategy and divisional technology strategy. I think she has given it more energy too, and more accountability. They did a terrific job."

I was not alone in exploring with Dasa and facing up to my own reality. There were many other colleagues in Corning's technology community who were also open to an intensive constructive feedback process and learned to find in themselves key characteristics of leadership. Dasa's challenge to us was "to be willing to integrate our inner and outer lives and to see our work as a place of making a meaningful living and encouraging individual fulfillment and freedom." Many were courageous enough to rise to the occasion and recognize the opportunities, and they were well on the path to authentic leadership. We were all learning together.

Whereas handling and maintaining efficient organizations requires good managerial efforts, creating impassioned organizations that can imagine the future, where individuals overcome all obstacles in pursuit of their inspiration and deliver breakthroughs that redefine reality, demands leadership that envisions possibilities, looks ahead, and foresees what is next. Leadership that does the right things sets the stage on which the amazing can and does occur. Whereas managers dwell in the world of the "how"—the practical, the details—leadership emphasizes the "why"—the values, the meaning, the purpose. Leaders emphasize identity, culture, and meaning; mobilize emotional and spiritual resources to motivate, inspire, nurture, and bring in the integral self; model the way; share power while remaining accountable for the success of the organization; and get people to *want* to do things. I discuss here some of the concepts I learned and lived as part of my practice, not as a discourse on the vast topic of leadership, which has received deep and inspiring treatments by the greats of Bill George, John Wooden, and others, but as a collection of the key elements and in the way I have experienced them as fundamental to genuine and authentic leadership.

At the core of genuine leadership is a clear sense of self-acceptance by the leader, which comes from strong and unrelenting work leading to self-awareness. These two qualities, self-acceptance and self-awareness, are the foundation of leadership as service that is expressed through courage, integrity, and empathy toward others, allowing a culture of empowerment to emerge.

EMPOWERMENT

There is a common temptation to view leadership as pushing really, really hard and wanting to go really, really fast. We feel at times that change can't ever be fast enough. But when the pursuit is for transformative change and the effort requires that each person put in the best of self day after day, the goal is achieved instead through revitalizing our organizations and shaping them in harmony with our values and deepest truths. Transformation is accomplished by creating meaningful, satisfying work for all involved, and conscious, healthy organizations; it is best realized by focusing on one person at a time, meeting unique needs with unique styles; and it can best be achieved by motivating people to take charge of their happiness, satisfaction, and high performance at work. As people in an organization take charge of their own satisfaction and performance, they experience the powerful force of living fulfillment through their work, which then transcends beyond being a daily activity to becoming a vehicle for the realization of individual potential.

The empowering stand of leading to bring out the best in others is about believing in people and being committed to their success and well-being. It is about seeing their potential—even before they do—and developing it, creating opportunities for them to walk into and grow, raising the bar and challenging people to stretch and expand, getting involved with those in your group in a two-way dialogue that provides them with rich feedback to foster growth even if it feels like an exposure of your own self, putting the mirror in front of them and leading them into a journey of self-discovery and awareness, though at times it may bring on pain. Ultimately, empowerment is based on a clear dialogue, and it results in an agreement embraced by all members that requires of the leader an openness to receive constructive feedback and critical review of her own work, and to be willing to change her views and actions in the light of new information.

It is this ultimate commitment between organization and leader that, by validating the process of distributing authority in the group and of encouraging accountability to release the full power of its members, defines empowering leadership. Though in abstract the concept of distributing authority may evoke images of weakness and debilitated influence, in reality this commitment has compelling sway in unleashing and driving high performance. Stemming from freedom and autonomy as experienced by all group members, this commitment yields an embrace of organizational strategy and a responsibility for self-motivation and accountability. Even the daily dynamics are touched and, as leadership functions are distributed throughout, empowerment becomes a game of co-creation where surprises occur and truly creative solutions are proposed. Ideas surface that otherwise would not see the light of day, the willingness and energy to make them happen swell, and individuals experience the power of their own driving force.

This game of co-creation allows the leader to bring into focus the true meaning of leadership: as a leader, your group members work *with* you, not *for* you. For the true meaning of leadership is one of service, guided by principles and values and focused on serving the large community and the well-being of others—the driving force behind performance. As leader you would thus be wise to declare this vision openly and frequently and to pair it with an affirmation of mission to serve and to support your group members in their fulfillment, to remind them that they do not work *for* you as leader but *with* you, and that you all work together for the benefit of the organization.

Leadership is a role of stewardship, of holding and developing the resources of the organization for the well-being of all. The concept of leadership as service may not be as ingrained in the general psyche as that of leadership as power. Power—the great illusion—is perhaps the characteristic most often identified with leadership, and the power of position, status, or authority is an attractive magnet for many. In authentic leadership, however, the true meaning of service is the translation of power from authority and position into responsibility for decisions that touch lives and affect careers, livelihoods, and the well-being of people in organizations. For leadership, the issue, then, is to discover how to use power wisely to make a difference with others and unleash and guide the driving forces within.

To have meaningful impact, leaders need to serve and touch lives one by one so the connection can be experienced individually. Even when addressing a large audience, the communication can be an intimate one between the leader and every person in the audience. In one-on-one situations, the approach and style need to be customized to each person, so that every member of your group gets from you the best guidance, the one personalized to his needs, the one that will bring out the best in him.

INTEGRITY

Integrity, acting consistently with who we are, what we stand for, and what we are here to do, is the defining value of authentic leadership. Being true to one's self necessitates a clear awareness of who we are and of our values, principles, and beliefs, and how we live them, from where it becomes the core of our personal strength.

Each one of our words and deeds is an expression of our integrity or the lack of it, and the concordance between them can easily be perceived by those around us. As in the case of empowerment, for integrity to spill out into the group a clear dialogue has to take place before an agreement can be embraced by all members. In the case of integrity, this agreement sets high expectations. A smart, empowered, impassioned group, encouraged to participate in the game of co-creation, will be observant of every action and word and unforgiving of any miscues from leadership. If they are met with openness and awareness, expressions of high expectations can play the invaluable role of "keeping the leader on his toes," and if they are responded to with candor and example, they can be the driver of organizational resilience.

Integrity has a profound effect on creating organizational power. It is the foundation for a deep sense of trust that drives high performance and morale; it supports organizational structure by clarifying roles and links, avoiding confusion and engendering cohesiveness and resilience; and, most significantly, as people are bonded by trust and respect for one another, integrity generates the soul of the organization. But in its path to becoming the soul, integrity is relentless in its demands. It needs to be by the side of leaders and group members alike as each one of them walks his talk, practices what he preaches, keeps promises, takes responsibility, and holds others accountable. It starts on day one of the role of leader, demanding that he declare his vision and live out the mission, that he be open in his communications, equipped with honesty and willingness to speak, and willing to provide appropriate constructive feedback, customized to the most important person—the one in front of him—in caring and supportive ways.

Staying true to our value of integrity is not always easy. In being true to our views and principles, the experience of stepping out with a bold proposal or unpopular stance, or of being honest with position and feedback, may provoke a scary feeling in leaders. We may perceive a sense of vulnerability or aggression as we face the risk of exposure, and our initial reaction may be an instinct to retreat to safety. But in staying true to ourselves we will find that the only true measure of integrity, our only true guide, is our own awareness of our consistency—and inconsistency—with our values and principles. The awareness of knowing when we are acting away from integrity *and coming back to it* is where our liberation stems from, as it becomes ultimately our strength and the source of our own invulnerability.

COURAGE

To live leadership with integrity and to follow the inner guidance of your values and principles is to live at risk. For most leaders the day-to-day life can lead to fear as they make big bets on new approaches, take unpopular stands, or say no to a boss, a customer, or an employee. Leaders who do not experience it this way have either learned to remain centered through deep awareness or are not pushing themselves beyond a safe comfort zone and are thus avoiding risk—and missing great opportunities. If not faced, these activity-related fears are reflected in an approach that holds leaders back from decisive action in the face of ambiguity, from sharing their vision and ultimately from choosing values over their self-interest—an approach that erodes group morale and esprit de corps.

Fear is not pointless. If it is met with awareness, it can be energizing. Though commonly regarded as the absence of fear, courage is rather the willingness to go right through fear. Courage is the readiness to feel the fear, see it, accept it without judgment, experience the sensation, and act anyway. The key to facing our fears and turning their power over us into energy behind us is to go deep within us, understand their roots, confront them, and let them go.

Many of our perceived risks stem from our need to attain or maintain a position that we hold dear. Thus making a bold proposal may risk our credibility or authority, taking an unpopular stand may risk acceptance by others, saying no to a boss may risk our career advancement. But just as the compass always points north, as long as we live in integrity we will know when we are out of it and how to reenter. In Peter Block's words, "If our primary goal is to move up the organization, then in most cases we will act with caution. If, however, our primary commitment is to contribute, to be of service to our users, treat people well, and maintain our integrity, then we are doomed to a course of adventure, uncertainty, and risk. In fact, the very obstacles we fear are there to help us discover our own integrity. Only when we push hard against others and they resist do we really know where we stand" (*The Empowered Manager,* San Francisco: Jossey-Bass, 1987).

In leadership, courage is not about suicidal stupidity, but about pairing awareness with wisdom and good judgment to develop organizational savvy, to know when and how to push—and how hard to push—to find allies and deliver results, to develop people and stand by them, to create cultures and defend them, to manage conflict, to demand excellence, and to do what it takes to enrich lives. Projects that deliver results considered unattainable, that create important strategic space for the business, are often started against all odds, with few supporters and nobody requesting them, but with the courage of an empowered organization behind them, an organization that knows it is needed and that follows the guidance of leadership who believes and insists that the goal can be achieved. For leadership in today's fast-paced world, the old-time maxim still holds: courage is about changing the things that can be changed and having the wisdom to know them from those that cannot.

EMPATHY

True leadership is marked by a commitment to the well-being and success of others rather than by an attraction to the mirage of control, power, and admiration. Having embraced service to others as the core, leadership provides an extraordinary opportunity to care for others and express it in tangible ways. An authentic leader is not only able to connect with her own emotions and manage them skillfully, but is also able to connect and identify with the feelings and emotions of others.

Whereas enthusiasm has been termed the emotion of high performance, empathy can be regarded as the emotion of empowerment. Offered together, empathy and enthusiasm are contagious drivers of inspiration. Given the strong macho dynamics of the workplace, it is not surprising that expressing concern and empathy for team members is still a risky, vulnerable practice for leaders, despite the acknowledgment of the significance of emotional intelligence in leadership. But empathy and enthusiasm are too powerful a force to be ignored in our efforts to create impassioned organizations where team members continuously put in their best for the good of the organization.

Going through the motions in following best practices and published tips on "how to help your workforce feel appreciated and loved" and how to improve retention rates is, at best, cheerleading. It is also transparent to a group of impassioned and unforgiving practitioners; genuine empathy cannot be faked. It is a leader's willingness to open the self to feel the excitement and pain and concern and hope of others, and to transfer and experience them as his own emotions, that is at the core of real motivation. This is not the purview of one gender over the other. What it takes is having sensitivity to the needs of others, respecting others, valuing and celebrating their differences, putting yourself in their shoes, and listening, listening, listening.

Empathy is expressed by valuing each individual, her potential and contribution, even if this means going out on a limb to create a new opportunity or to champion an unorthodox candidate and putting yourself at risk. It means believing in your people and regarding them as able and giving them space and support even when their ideas are orthogonal to yours and their style is at odds with that of the organization. Empathy requires being able to see the fire inside and finding a fit, even if the change is ahead of their dreams or makes them apprehensive, as well as knowing them past their reserved faces to envision their potential. It also means wanting them to feel so good about themselves that they won't need to punch somebody else in order to attain that feeling. But empathy does not mean having a Pollyannaish view or approach; it does not mean sanitizing the world so that they can feel good, or taking away a personality that somebody does not work well with. It means, rather, raising the bar for them to learn to develop the self-awareness that will allow them to deal with those difficult personalities, for if they don't face their nemeses now, they will encounter them again later. Empathy, in sum, is about empowering and generating vast possibilities that are unique for each individual.

There is a deeper dimension to empathy that puts further demands on the leader, as empathy is not just about caring for others but also about giving of self. It is about sharing of self in commitment to service, your commitment to grow and develop people through coaching and mentoring. Living in both integrity and empathy exacts an openness and transparency about our own experience that not only is enriching but also raises the bar for those around us. It means giving of self not only in real time and energy investments, but additionally in the sharing of experiences, vulnerability, and wisdom. This may feel risky, as if revealing our rich experiences, broken dreams, past attempts, and failures somehow exposes our vulnerability. But it is not only an opportunity to walk undaunted right through our own fear, but to open a world of learning that would otherwise remain unattainable. The greatest richness, though, comes from our own example of courage, in the sharing, in the awareness of our own feelings, and in the willingness to express them. As for the leader, the richness comes from having the opportunity to serve, and this is truly priceless.

Ultimately, the maximum expression of commitment to the success and well-being of the people in your group is when a leader embraces their success and expects grander things for them than for himself. For the leader this emerges from a deep sense of self-awareness and requires him to work through feelings of competitiveness and ambition and remain focused on the spirit of service.

FUN AND PLAY

The commitment of a leader to the well-being of others cannot stop outside of herself. The commitment to others, rather, needs to start with a commitment by the leader to care for herself as trustee of the energy and balance required to ensure the success of others. Having embraced service to others as the core, leadership demands the safeguarding of the physical and mental fortitude of the leader herself.

Balance your life, we hear often. And for leaders, this is not just a need, but a bond. Just as a powerful engine needs high-octane fuel, the spirit of leadership needs a source of energy, one that resides outside of work. Activities that move you away from the daily fray, that by allowing you to access your inner knowing and the flow of your intuition release withheld emotions and allow you to remain centered and to manage stress, will bring that balance and restore your ability to face situations and to lead. To lead with continued gusto, with energy, with passion and excitement. After all, it is from a healthy ability to stay at your center that the true rest and revitalization needed for productive work comes.

Fun and play allow a litheness to move in and bring back that peaceful space that is often lost in the intensity of the day. So if you do not already have them, allow your dreams to take you for a ride and find activities to liberate your spirit in ways that are fulfilling to you, activities that you *love* to do, those that take you away from the reality of the day and make you lose track of the passage of time, that restore your sense of vitality and your enthusiasm for living. Develop interests and skills that allow your creativity to flow, activities that keep your body fit, and practices that keep you balanced. And defend, ardently, the time to devote to them. The quality of your life, the fullness of your leadership experience, the well-being of others, will all be the better for it.

SELF-AWARENESS

Throughout our lives we develop a notion of self that defines us through our roles, credentials, and occupation and that is couched in our values, principles, and beliefs. This is the part of the self that deals with the positions we take and the decisions we make on a daily basis, a part of the self familiar to us. Through conditioning from our life experience, this part of the self reacts with the emotion of the moment—urgency, delight, indignation, anger. It is the aggregate of these reactions that we have come to identify as our self, the external expression. At our core, however, resides that quality inherent in the wisdom of our true nature, that part of us that knows without knowing and is unruffled by experience, a quality we seldom reach. As leaders we need to let it flow out, for to abide in it is to operate without the limitations that keep this power, the power that knows, that intuits, that feels, hidden.

Like the need of the creative being to be shielded from the daily busy-ness and mental clutter that keep him from accessing his best "I-don't-know-why" ideas, our intuitive knowledge is revealed in the silence of no thought. Mindfulness, the art of giving full attention to thoughts, feelings, and behaviors that are taking place at the moment, at each moment, and moment by moment, frees up the space for intuition to flow and is the key to all appropriate response. Mindfulness brings a capacity for penetrating clarity, a way of seeing things as they really are, that has tremendous power. And when true reality emerges, a leader can understand the situation in its entirety. From this awareness of what is really happening evolves the detachment that provides a leader with his strongest suit: the understanding that his energy yields its greatest output when it goes into caring and developing, not into controlling, and that it is his participation, not his control, that is required. It is this realization that allows leaders to stay centered and feel fulfillment through hail and storm.

In order to resolve outer conflict, leaders must be able to resolve their inner conflict first, and this cannot be achieved without self-knowledge. Thoughts, feelings, and unconscious behaviors control you until you notice them. Once you notice your own patterns, you have the power to deal with them. Ultimately, freedom comes from seeing clearly through the fundamental conditioning beliefs behind our desires, feelings, and emotions. Awareness is seeing underneath our actions, habits, and patterns and seeing the beliefs that feed those desires and emotions. Only when you see clearly what fuels your emotions can you accept them and let them go, or change them. And only then can you truly understand that the lone change you can effect is to your own actions and reactions. Likewise, the changes you wish to impose on others are only theirs to effect. Your role as a leader is to support your people in a process of awareness similar to the one you follow so that they, too, can move away from being the unconscious mechanical actors of their life experience and learn to have the choice to respond appropriately.

From early on in our lives, our conditioning and programming inform our perception of leadership, and for many of us this perception comes with a burden of authority associated with the need to be right. As leaders, we then grow to act in accord with the position and to want to be right at all times. Only when we see our desire to be right for what it is will we understand that the willingness to accept being wrong is a courageous stand and the foundation for change and learning.

Similarly, leaders are often beleaguered by desires identified with leadership—success, acclaim, influence, authority, control, fame, fortune, relationships, status—and their leadership experience becomes one of repeating actions that result in the pleasing reaction. But as wiser leaders find out and history attests, gratification of the desire does not create satisfaction. The bottom line on desire is that desire itself is never satisfied; the *process* of desire goes on and on. The only way to break the cycle is the realization that satisfaction is *within* the self, that only the *absence* of desire brings satisfaction. And, once again, only when we have the awareness of what is behind our actions, when through self-awareness we gain the ability to recognize what has power over us in our everyday experience, are we free to choose and eliminate the desire.

The other side of the coin of desire is, of course, fear of not having what we desire. Leaders are often haunted by the fear of failure, of being exposed, of being wrong, of appearing weak, of lack of control, of rejection, of loss or criticism. The mirror image of what we desire is what we often fear. If we desire approval and acclaim, we fear rejection; if we crave success, we dread failure and risk; if power has a strong hold on us, being controlled frightens us; if our game is about winning, the idea of losing scares us. Understanding the power of this polarity helps us release our grip on fear, and awareness gives us the choice to respond appropriately and to put our power in the direction we choose.

Self-awareness is an imperative for leadership. You need to discover who you are before you can lead others, before you can help them, and before they will trust you. Conversely, the many dimensions and facets of leadership, the many different situations and challenges awakening unconscious conditioning and eliciting emotional responses in you, create an unparalleled opportunity for self-discovery, inner growth, and fulfillment.

SELF-ACCEPTANCE

The quality of self-confidence that allows leaders to live in integrity and courage differs from the subtle trap of pride and arrogance that may accompany the role of leader. The former stems from self-awareness and the realization that leadership is about serving others to feel fulfilled and reach their potential, whereas the latter is based on the ability of the status and power of the leadership position to inflate one's sense of self. When trusting this shiny fairy-tale mirror, any self-doubt about one's inherent value or capabilities pushes us to look outside ourselves for the recognition, appreciation, and worth we may fear we lack. This struggle to cement a sense of worth by proving that we are better, bigger, stronger, is behind most ego battles—whether in the workplace, the boardroom, or the middle school playground. The danger for leadership lies in using the power to quiet the pain brought by the nagging doubt of unworthiness, and this is an addictive cycle.

Courage, then, lies in not using the power of leadership as your fix for feeling good about yourself. The service of authentic leadership is the diametric opposite of the fix. Leadership as service transcends this ego trap and serves the well-being of others *without an agenda* of self-aggrandizement.

The confidence gained by the leader as she experiences the shift from self-focus and struggle for survival, fame, position, and recognition to one of full contribution to work and life is a crucial source of inspiring leadership and morale. This shift, an outgrowth of a profound process of self-discovery, has a lasting effect on performance, though it requires ruthless honesty and persistence all along the way. It asks for acceptance of your total being and behavior: acceptance of your skills and your needs, your joys and your breakdowns, your strengths and your foibles, your performance on and off the stage, even when you hate it. Self-acceptance is not about lowering the bar for yourself, but rather about allowing your commitment to excellence to emerge without the tension found in striving for perfection. It is self-acceptance that distinguishes the high performer from the perfectionist; it drives self-improvement while shying away from the debilitating effects of self-judgment. This continuous drive for increased performance takes courage while freeing up energy that boosts motivation and stimulation, allowing the focus to shift from "me and my needs" to "them and theirs."

Leadership as service can only come through nonjudgmental acceptance of your whole being, regardless of your behavior and perceived lacks. Self-acceptance brings humility, which in turn frees us from arrogance and the drive to inflate ourselves. Leadership as service flourishes when there is no personal agenda of acquisition, when the leader is free to serve and to lead with the best interests of others at heart, while releasing the need to prove himself to be above or below others.

Dasa summarizes this state of leadership in a powerful way when he says, "This shift in self-concept is key to enlightened leadership. It frees you from the need to be right and in control, from abusing power and position, and feeding on admiration. It allows you to focus on others rather than yourself, to authentically empower others without your own agenda interfering. You are able to give people credit, allow them to be visible and stand out, without fear of being overshadowed. It allows you to serve" (Let Davidson, *Wisdom at Work*, Burdett, N.Y.: Larson Publications, 1998).

Let Life Continue

I HAD BEEN ON TOP OF THE WORLD. My husband and I have always enjoyed hiking, and climbing to the summit of mountains has always held a particular attraction, so regardless of the continent, when the two of us are together it is mountains rather than cities that we visit. This last expedition, the one that put us on top of Mount Kilimanjaro, had been an unforgettable trip that had pushed us to new feelings. In five days of climbing we saw the lush tropical rain forest at the base of the mountain replaced by shrubs and grasses, and then by the unusual giant groundsels in the misty moorlands of higher elevations before it would completely disappear, replaced by a Martian vastness where only the ring of sharp volcanic rock shards punctuated our steps. We had gotten to understand our own limits, and it had left an indelible mark on us.

"Pole, pole," our guide had stressed all along in Swahili. "Slowly, slowly," we had climbed for most of the mountain, and never more so than at the final stage, where the air was at its thinnest and the solid ground had been replaced by a fine gray volcanic ash that shifted under our boots. We moved up at a steady pace, making progress in silence, each one with his thoughts, guided by the light of a magic full moon. Then just before dawn we reached the summit and slowly the valley underneath opened up, the trace of faraway mountains reappearing on the horizon. The mountain came alive, the glaciers sharing their delicate hues of whites and aquas and lilacs as the sun hit them. It was only then that we understood what it means to be on top of the world—and what it takes.

And in life I was feeling on top of the world. There are moments when life seems to enjoy smiling at you. I had had a couple of those years in France. Though living by myself in a new country, I had enjoyed the challenge and the independence of this foreign assignment. The new strategic direction of the lab was well received by upper management, its implementation had touched the lives of people in a positive way, and there was an air of excitement and motivation that was palpable to all, residents and visitors. My children, now graduate students back in the United States, were now terrific adults, and we enjoyed watching them develop and having them join us for vacations in Europe.

I had returned to headquarters, rewarded by joining the ranks of corporate VPs—again breaking the proverbial glass ceiling—and I was exploring new areas for me and new markets for Corning's technologies. I was physically fit and energized by my finish, second place for my age group, in the first triathlon of what I was planning would be many to come. Life was busy, "good busy"; we were all healthy and happy.

But life had a change in store for me. After all, as Buddhist philosophy would put it, life is what happens when one is busy making plans. A month after my first triathlon and 366 days after my previous mammogram, my test turned out to be "not normal." Further biopsies and tests would show that, contrary to my feeling of well-being over the past year, I had a very aggressive form of breast cancer that had rapidly spread to my lymphatic system. I had a stage three cancer with several large, heavily matted and adhered tumors that were inoperable unless they reacted to strong doses of chemotherapy, and a mere 15 percent chance of a full recovery.

The "dose dense" chemotherapy that I was to receive would drain my energy to levels unbeknownst to me. I had days when I was unable to hold a magazine up to read or even bring the spoon to my mouth to eat. So staying in shape during this time—and for a long time to come—no longer meant my daily routine of swimming laps or lifting weights or going for a jog or for a bike ride with my husband, but simply taking the dogs on walks, long ones at first, becoming shorter as my energy dropped.

Somehow, inexplicably, I was spared. If somebody were to ask me what worked, like all the medical doctors and researchers who work hard at unleashing the facts, I could not point out any one thing—from drugs to determination to strength to concentration to creative forces—but to a circle of things that makes up the totality of the experience. It had been an excruciatingly difficult experience, but a beautiful experience nonetheless.

I was yet to receive the life-restoring news that my postsurgery biopsy had detected no cancer cells left in me when I received what felt like a blow directly to my abdomen at a moment when life had already kicked me to the ground. Two days after my last dose of chemotherapy, at my darkest and weakest moment, when I was feeling that I had no more energy left to lose, my boss came to pay me a visit at home. He had done this a couple of times in the past four months, and I had always had the strength to meet him in our living room. This time I was not able to get out of bed, and he sat on a chair by my bedside. He explained that economic conditions were forcing Corning to go through a reduction in workforce, that he was having to choose among his employees, and that an early retirement package would be offered to eligible employees. Though not able to remember specifics at that moment, the agony that leaders experience under those circumstances was easy for me to relive. I remembered myself having to choose from among the best and deciding how the group could survive without some of them. I remembered, too, the need to choose the wording, the intonation, the modulation, and the timbre so that the message, the offer of "voluntary early retirement," would be received with the intended intention: "No, you do not have to retire, we want to keep you" for some, and "Are you really telling me that you want me to retire?" for others.

I thought at first that he had come to me for input, as I still was responsible for many of the people in his group. It caught me off guard when, instead, I heard him extending the offer of early retirement to me, repeatedly stating that he wanted to give me the greatest freedom. "But I did not think that corporate officers were eligible for this round of early retirement," was all that I could muster. I continued to express that my utmost freedom would come from his unyielding support, that I had viewed going back to work as my next summit to conquer. After a short while I had no more energy left in me for discussion.

It was hard not to share this news with my children, but I did not want this development to overwhelm our Christmas that year, coming a week later. My chemo, my upcoming mastectomy, my chances for survival, were already affecting us enough. My family would first witness in disbelief my inability to fight, to look for another position in the corporation, to discuss it with senior leadership. But I was not giving in, and they stood by me. The fighter in me, the one they were used to seeing charging and resisting and driving for causes with passion, though weakened by the struggle, was charging on another front, focused on survival. All I appeared to do was lie listless in bed, drifting in and out of sleep, as my life changed. But I had understood the importance of staying centered on the battle most significant to me, the one for my life. The corporate battle receded. I knew the people I could call. I knew what other positions I could hold. I knew whose support I had in the corporation. But the sheer thought of scheduling appointments and making my case, of getting out of bed, of getting dressed in corporate garb, of putting the colorful turbans and large earrings and makeup that months before I had sported, was exhausting and confusing, a distraction for my concentration and my vanishing vigor. I saved my energy for the important battle. My strength came from feeling my family—my children, my husband, my sisters and nieces—right by my side, regardless of the outcome, and my serenity from truly embracing Dasa's teachings and accepting what came, recovery, illness, death, or early retirement. Reconstructing my life, however, would later test me further.

Putting your life together after a strong cancer experience can be quite disconcerting. In the aftermath of my illness and my retirement from Corning, there was a sense of emptiness in me, a sense of not knowing what awaited me. But there was not a feeling of apprehension, as I also intuited that there was to be another stage to my life. The drugs, the determination, the confrontation with death, the acceptance, had all brought changes to the person I was. Not only would I have to learn who this new person was, but I would have to do it without the railings that life puts by our sides as we walk it: our work, our relationships to those that have been a part of our daily life. After attempting to pick up where I had left off by following some of the daily routines I was used to, I understood that I now had a new energy I needed to become familiar with, understand, and allow to flow. I then realized that I had to teach myself, to reinvent myself, that I would have to look at myself, understand my creative flow, and give myself the space to unleash it. I would have to create a new context where my passion could take flight. I had to lead myself in the same way I had passionately led others. I needed to turn around my passion for inspiring others to deliver breakthroughs and apply it to myself.

Understanding myself as a creative being, how I could set my energy free, and what would the activities be that would allow me to bring my whole self in was, of course, paramount. Of all my options—weaving, surface design, sewing and other aspects of textile art, painting, consulting, or writing—where did it mean most for me to put my energy? Memories of how I had led different people would come to mind—the fiery drive of Peter Murray versus the equanimity of Dave Johnson—as did the patience I had had toward them when I would become impatient with myself; the constant revisiting of American culture and the exploration of its language in helping Jiabao Lu, the hard-driven, fearless scientist and abstract thinker from mainland China, understand that his brutally honest and "less than subtle" ways were not only poorly received but were ineffective; the intensive game of letting out rope and taking it in as Manuel Cáceres, the talented musician and manager, learned the balance between "being his own man" and being an effective leader in an organization. The recollections were both inspiring and demanding of me. I played at painting and trying new techniques. I explored sewing with new fabrics and making garments that pushed me. Insisting on excellence has been a part of me, and I would rework a piece of silk on an exacting gown until I was satisfied while at the same time learning to be gentle with myself.

Learning the new rhythms of my energy was also important. I was used to being a dynamo that would fire at five in the morning, start the day with a good physical workout, and take it from there. I would be starving before noontime and had to refuel then, and then again in the early evening. But one, two years after chemo, my body asked for a different rhythm, one that was new to me, and before I could allow myself this new rhythm, I had to remember how I had been supportive of those creatives that came in late in the morning. So I learned to go through long work sessions starting in the midmorning and continuing uninterrupted until midafternoon, when I would break the spell of my creative flow and realize that I needed a bite to eat. The image of those night-owl creatives whose energy would not awaken until midmorning and whose cycle they honored and was given space by a culture of flexible work hours would come to me: Paul Genetti, the independent research fellow who had no need for managers, stopping at lunchtime for his hour of self-organized volleyball games; or Brian MacHarg, the corduroy and Adidas indoor soccer shoes scientist who had to push himself hard to make it to meetings at 8:30 A.M. but would be the last one to leave the building at night; or Isabel Lopez, the multitalented fluorine chemist whose energy waned in the winter months with the intensity of the sun and who responded to a few days at lower latitudes. And I responded by understanding that I did not have to measure myself with my old yardstick and that I could give my new self the space to be.

Figuring out the structure that my day needed to be productive while at the same time agreeing with this new cycling of my energy was one of the greatest challenges for me as I regained my work life. It eluded me for a while, as I consulted with other friends who had recently retired. Though they had not experienced the health assault on their bodies, I figured they had also experienced the jump from an overly structured life to one that lacks any structure at all, but they were just as baffled as I was. I thought back to the importance of structure for groups chartered with delivering through their creativity and found myself feeling what I had heard Kirsten and Peter and Tim and Rabbindrana ask for: a culture of creative engagement and liberating values, where there is open space to be intuitive and follow the inner drive, one that coexists with a clear definition of structure—roles, links, responsibilities, and, for me, structure to my days, to my weeks.

I was reminded of the significance of the leader as an active participant in clearing activity clutter and distraction, in eschewing frenetic work habits and overwork, in supporting an organizational structure where creativity and passionate exploration coexist with clear definition of organization and schedule, where there are boundaries that provide guidance that create space and liberate passions. So I learned to appreciate the value of creating days that start late, with activities that engage my creative side for uninterrupted long blocks of time, that follow with late afternoon lunches, and that end up with a session of physical activity. In other words, an unconventional day structure that radically contradicted my previous decades of experience. I relished in the experience and balanced my need for a clean and organized workspace at the outset of a project with my tendency to have all my fabrics, or my paintings or my reference papers, scattered around my studio where I can easily find them in the middle of a project, by learning from my own understanding of Peter Murray's Archaean-to-Recent stratigraphic column of a desk. And I plowed through with rigor and discipline, staying at it when the work called more for completion than for creation.

It was when I started writing that I truly got a taste for the intuitive flow. After months of toying with one activity and another, after unfulfilled offers by friends and other consultants, and rejections by speaker bureaus because of my lack of publications on the subject, I went back to find my true passion. I recalled the many times I would encourage those in my groups to recognize when life is not flowing and that by insisting on a given path, one is simply hitting one's head against the wall, when all that is needed is to stop in your tracks and look elsewhere for the door that opens. This realization, and becoming aware of the energy and passion I exuded as I talked about my leadership experiences, gave me the energy to sit down and write about them. No specific goal in mind drove me, only the need to chronicle it. Sitting down in a beautiful setting surrounded by tropical rain forest, high mountains, and serenading birds, I tuned into the flow. I would write for hours, stopping only when the flow stopped, and then going for a walk in the garden or for a few laps in the swimming pool. And in those carefree moments, when all I was focused on was the quality of the stroke as the arm hit the water, the new bird attracted to the ripe plantain on the bird feeder, or the number of new buds in an orchid plant, the thought or the structure or the paragraph that had eluded me would just appear. I could then go back to the keyboard—sometimes having to race back before an idea escaped me, at other times with such a clear picture of what was coming that it remained vivid in me for hours—and move on. But there was no forcing it. There would be times when that same intuition would make it clear that it was time to stop; "I am not coming through now," I would hear. The recollection of moments when I had seen a scientist "on a roll" was hard to escape. Physicist and ballroom dancer Tim Cobb as he dove into compaction models for glass; butterfly catcher Brian MacHarg and his insistence on pursuing an understanding of oxide-free glasses; gourmet cook Dave Johnson revving up the Bugatti engine of his creative mind when the problem at hand demanded it; my own experiences as a young scientist. And I was thankful to have understood that for them, to have respected it and protected it for them then, and for myself now.

I could feel then the creative process flowing unfettered. It was a joy, and I was relishing the activity, but to see something materialize out of it, I understood that writing was only the beginning. I needed to create the team of readers and experts to react to the text, opine, endorse, contradict, value, guide. I needed to engage talent with differing approaches and personalities, different experiences and stages in life, but shared values and shared passion for leadership and innovation issues. And the hardest part, because I had no responsibility for any of them and even less for a team of them, was to ask them to give me excellence as well as discipline out of their sheer good nature; how can you be exacting of somebody who is simply giving you as a gift their time on top of their expertise?

The answer was actually simple. I could be exacting the same way I was for the creatives for whom I had had responsibility and whom I had brought together into teams: by knowing and understanding them, their rhythms, their uniqueness, and by treating each one of them with the individuality that each represents, the respect that each one finds meaningful. By celebrating their idiosyncrasies, by asking them to do the right mission for their skills, just as my knowledge of my GLBT coach Kirsten Steinmeier's skills and background had allowed me to make the assignment that restored production overnight to an otherwise handicapped plant, or the understanding of Jeff Major's technical and functional experience allowed us to find the person to lead a multipersonnel, multitechnology search for a diesel filter for Europe that would have made many a project leader dizzy.

So I would tread lightly, understanding the complexity of their work, their travel schedules, the demands on their lives, and asking for the gift of their insight and their views. Asking them specific questions that would honor their experience, their uniqueness in a field, even their age group—the recent MBA graduate could offer me a unique insight, as could the author of renown, the leading consultant, or the university professor. Knowing when to expect a written critique, when to take notes furiously over the phone as their mind and words raced, and when to come down to the city or fly across the country for a personal visit. My only hope was that through my writings and our exchanges I would be able to offer insights that would enrich their lives and experience in one way or another and, by so doing, provide motivation and thirst for knowledge as their biggest reward, a lesson I had learned repeatedly from creatives.

And so my writing project started to come to life, and with it the energy and passion that I was used to experiencing when leading creative talent, started to emerge, marred only by the shadow of my internal struggle with my retirement, which would come back, unannounced, to haunt me. And in those moments, the recollection of those whom I had encouraged to engage in an exploration into self-awareness, the most powerful tool in a leader's box of tricks when managing conflict, would come to me. Peter Murray, the hot fire of creativity whose forceful ways mixed with his deep understanding of science left little room for others; Wendy Li's search for inner fortitude and its translation into effective demeanor; Sebastian Estephe's powerful assessment of dreams and roles. I knew then that I had only one recourse: to continue to relentlessly pursue this exploration into self-awareness. To understand, as I had encouraged others, that the only person I could change was myself, my beliefs, my behaviors. Though Dasa was gone—having succumbed to an aggressive cancer eighteen months after my diagnosis—I would continue living his teachings, knowing that I had to let go of the dream and accept reality, to push further into self-awareness and move on to self-acceptance. Only then could my energy flow back through me with vigor. Only then could I attempt to live the elements of genuine leadership. I was learning to embrace my own private conflict and turn it into a creative force.

As with my healing experience, I got the picture, very much as I had been aware through the passionate experience of leading teams, that what succeeds is not one thing, but a circle of things all working in harmony. As I immersed myself in rich discussions with the leadership practitioners and consultants and authors and journalists and editors and graduate students that were now my guiding team on the elements of creating cultures where innovation thrives, my eagerness and anticipation to jump back into action was tangible. Years after my time with the glass research group, my learning about the Society Committed to Relaxation, spurred by Tim Cobb, loner fundamental physicist turned unmasked ballroom dancer and gregarious mentor, cemented the notion that one can indeed create a culture that prevails, passed down through generations by oral tradition and rituals of celebration, not through top-to-bottom corporate efforts, but within the intimacy of a single group, one person at a time. I understood that what I needed to do, as I had done before, was bring the vital elements—the *passions*—together to work as a unit, prodding here, cajoling there, so they all resonate as one:

- To jump into the ring of fire and embrace the conflict that inevitably arises as the different experiences and viewpoints of creatives emerge as different ideas, often opposing and driven, at times violently, by the energy that fuels them.

- To bring passionate, brilliant, and creative people together who show a vibrancy in their personal lives, and whose interests, skills, and collaborations will create the persona of the group.

- To define values that resonate with you as a leader and that are both conducive to the expansion of the creative spirit and to the spirit of excellence and rigor that is paramount in taking visions and dreams to physical reality.

- To demand excellence and enrich lives by coaxing individuals and teams to let their intuition and drive guide them while instilling a spirit of high performance and focusing on commitment to make it happen.

- To create a culture of creative engagement within the intimacy of a single group, one defined by beliefs, attitudes, energy, interaction style, and practices.

- To define a clear structure, one that will inform the interactions, the roles and the responsibilities of every single person and, in so doing, will eliminate barriers and frustrations and provide every one with a raison d'être.

- To develop the self-awareness and acceptance that allows you as a leader to stay centered, to be impassioned and detached, and in so doing to be motivational and inspirational on one hand, and to guide the raft through whitewater on the other.

It finally became clear, as I had intuited earlier, that there is another stage ahead, a new phase to my life. I also understood my cancer to be that unassailable force that came to turn my life around and place it along a new path, at a point in life where I would not have changed myself. My textile art will continue to be an important creative outlet for me—and I may even continue to explore others. But my passion, my way of bringing my whole self in, is by creating cultures where innovation thrives. So now I enter the stage of guiding and counseling others on how to create these cultures in their own settings and organizations rather than doing it myself in a group of my own, teaching them to unleash the magic of innovation by liberating creativity and guiding it to deliver innovation, counseling them on how to balance creativity with rigor and excellence, how to create cultures that create and deliver breakthroughs. In different settings and different cultures but, always, one person at a time.

ACKNOWLEDGMENTS

THIS BOOK WAS INCUBATED along my course of years of leading bright and challenging creatives to follow their own path. It is to them, who put their trust in—or rebelled against—my guidance, and *some* of whose stories are narrated here, that I owe my gratitude. Without them and their stories, this book would not have been possible. You all know who you are, but the world may not need to. To each one of you I bow my head in appreciation. For me, it was Dasarath Davidson who provided the guidance and teachings that changed my life in wonderful ways, and to whom I will always be indebted.

Occurrences in life often rely on catalysts to materialize, and it was only after receiving wings of motivation from Cheryl De Ciantis, who made me aware of the energy and passion that I exuded as I talked about my experiences in leading to liberate creativity, in creating cultures of innovation, that I found the energy to chronicle my learnings. Without her nudging encouragement, my practice and savoir faire might have remained as just a special memory for me to cherish.

I was fortunate to be surrounded by a group of experts, writers, and leadership researchers who guided me along from early in the writing to later in the editing. Cheryl De Ciantis, Chris Bergonzi, Charles O'Reilly, and Charles Fishman stood by me all along, with insightful expertise, honest critiques, and the beautiful gift of time and sustenance of spirit.

The insight of Kenton Hyatt, Lisa Chacón, Peter Bocko, Robert Kaiser, Robert Burnside, Bob Kaplan, Robert Thomas, and Emilio De Lia on earlier versions of the manuscript and their evaluation and advice on the richness versus the gratuitous, the established versus the new expanded and challenged me. The voice of a younger generation eager for experiences in leadership came to me through Andrew Marshall, Christina Brown-Marshall, and Jay Newman, who with their fresh graduate degrees and professional experiences enriched my view with their perspective, my text with their questions.

I am grateful to have been raised in a spirit of believing that *nothing* in life is impossible, an attitude that has carried me along and that I owe to both my parents and my siblings, who shared with me the making of the canvas of life. Bob Coleman, with his steady belief in me, has shored my own, and the spirit of my children, Colin and Maia, has animated and inspired my days. And, of course, along my longer years in leading and my shorter ones in writing, it has been my husband Bruce, whose quiet and unwavering support has always been by me.

INDEX

ABOUT THE AUTHOR

LINA ECHEVERRÍA spent twenty-five years inspiring creativity and accelerating innovation at Corning Incorporated, one of America's leading technology companies.

Echeverría led teams of scientists and researchers at Corning that developed everything from the ceramic filters for car exhausts, glasses for TV screens, dental bridges, and dinnerware. She was part of a culture that has provided the world with everything from the optical fiber that is the backbone of the Internet to the glass used as the tough but beautiful touchscreen for iPhones.

At Corning, Echeverría created an environment where scientists were both creative and productive, where teams balanced the ability to explore the edges of possibility, while also delivering critical new technology on time and on budget. Echeverría was known not just for her ability to effectively lead and manage (and keep happy) creative scientists, she was known for her ability to teach those skills to other managers. During her career, she managed teams and led organizations both in Corning, New York, and in Fontainebleau, France.

Echeverría began challenging convention early, as a student in her native Colombia. She was the first woman to seek admission and to graduate with a degree in engineering geology from the Universidad Nacional de Colombia at Medellín, opening the door to a new field for a generation of women in a school with a tradition as the most rigorous in the country in engineering. She went on to earn a Ph.D. in geology at Stanford.

After winning a fight against aggressive breast cancer, Echeverría stepped aside from the corporate world to focus on her passions: helping create cultures of innovation inside companies and organizations, and creating wearable textile art in her studio. The mother of two children, she is fluent in English, Spanish, and French, and has lived in four different countries. She lives in upstate New York with her husband, also a research scientist, and their two greyhounds.

Learn more at www.linaecheverria.com.